T0353211

HARRIET LANE

Harriet Lane's debut *Alys, Always* was longlisted for the Authors' Club Best First Novel Award and shortlisted for the Writers' Guild Best Fiction Book Award. Her second novel *Her* was selected for the Waterstones Book Club and shortlisted for the Encore Award for best second novel. She has worked as an editor and staff writer at *Tatler* and the *Observer*, and has also written for the *Guardian*, *Vogue* and the *New York Times*.

LUCINDA COXON

Lucinda Coxon's plays include *Herding Cats* at Hampstead Theatre; *What Are They Like?*, *The Eternal Not* and *Happy Now?* (Writers' Guild of Great Britain Best Play Award 2008, Drama Desk and Lortel Award nomination) at the National Theatre; *Nostalgia* and *Vesuvius* for South Coast Rep; *Improbabilities* at Soho Poly; *Wishbones* and *Waiting at the Water's Edge* at the Bush. Her stage adaptations include *The Shoemaker's Incredible Wife* from Federico García Lorca and *The Ice Palace* from the novel by Tarjei Vesaas, both for National Theatre Connections. Screenplays include the Oscar-winning *The Danish Girl*, *The Little Stranger*, *Wild Target*, *The Heart of Me*. Television includes BAFTA-nominated *The Crimson Petal and the White*.

Other Titles in this Series

Annie Baker
THE FLICK
JOHN

Mike Bartlett
ALBION
BULL
GAME
AN INTERVENTION
KING CHARLES III
SNOWFLAKE
WILD

Chris Bush
THE ASSASSINATION OF
    KATIE HOPKINS
STEEL

Lucinda Coxon
HAPPY NOW?
HERDING CATS

Jez Butterworth
THE FERRYMAN
JERUSALEM
JEZ BUTTERWORTH PLAYS: ONE
MOJO
THE NIGHT HERON
PARLOUR SONG
THE RIVER
THE WINTERLING

Caryl Churchill
BLUE HEART
CHURCHILL PLAYS: THREE
CHURCHILL PLAYS: FOUR
CHURCHILL PLAYS: FIVE
CHURCHILL: SHORTS
CLOUD NINE
DING DONG THE WICKED
A DREAM PLAY *after* Strindberg
DRUNK ENOUGH TO SAY
    I LOVE YOU?
ESCAPED ALONE
FAR AWAY
HERE WE GO
HOTEL
ICECREAM
LIGHT SHINING IN
    BUCKINGHAMSHIRE
LOVE AND INFORMATION
MAD FOREST
A NUMBER
PIGS AND DOGS
SEVEN JEWISH CHILDREN
THE SKRIKER
THIS IS A CHAIR
THYESTES *after* Seneca
TRAPS

debbie tucker green
BORN BAD
DIRTY BUTTERFLY
EAR FOR EYE
HANG
NUT
A PROFOUNDLY AFFECTIONATE,
PASSIONATE DEVOTION TO
    SOMEONE (– *NOUN*)
RANDOM
STONING MARY
TRADE & GENERATIONS
TRUTH AND RECONCILIATION

Sam Holcroft
COCKROACH
DANCING BEARS
EDGAR & ANNABEL
PINK
RULES FOR LIVING
THE WARDROBE
WHILE YOU LIE

Vicky Jones
THE ONE
TOUCH

Anna Jordan
CHICKEN SHOP
FREAK
POP MUSIC
THE UNRETURNING
YEN

Lucy Kirkwood
BEAUTY AND THE BEAST
    with Katie Mitchell
BLOODY WIMMIN
THE CHILDREN
CHIMERICA
HEDDA *after* Ibsen
IT FELT EMPTY WHEN THE
    HEART WENT AT FIRST BUT
    IT IS ALRIGHT NOW
LUCY KIRKWOOD PLAYS: ONE
NSFW
TINDERBOX

Rose Lewenstein
COUGAR
DARKNET
FUCKING FEMINISTS
NOW THIS IS NOT THE END

Clare McIntyre
LOW LEVEL PANIC
MY HEART'S A SUITCASE
    & LOW LEVEL PANIC
THE MATHS TUTOR
THE THICKNESS OF SKIN

Sam Potter
HANNA

Holly Robinson
SOFT ANIMALS

Jack Thorne
2ND MAY 1997
BUNNY
BURYING YOUR BROTHER IN
    THE PAVEMENT
A CHRISTMAS CAROL *after* Dickens
HOPE
JACK THORNE PLAYS: ONE
JUNKYARD
LET THE RIGHT ONE IN
    after John Ajvide Lindqvist
MYDIDAE
THE SOLID LIFE OF SUGAR WATER
STACY & FANNY AND FAGGOT
WHEN YOU CURE ME
WOYZECK *after* Büchner

Phoebe Waller-Bridge
FLEABAG

Joe White
MAYFLY

Lucinda Coxon

ALYS, ALWAYS

Based on the novel by
Harriet Lane

NICK HERN BOOKS
London
www.nickhernbooks.co.uk

A Nick Hern Book

This stage adaptation of *Alys, Always* first published in Great Britain in 2019 as a paperback original by Nick Hern Books Limited, The Glasshouse, 49a Goldhawk Road, London W12 8QP

Front cover image: Art Direction: Michael Mayhew; Photographer: Hugo Glendinning

Designed and typeset by Nick Hern Books, London
Printed in Great Britain by Mimeo Ltd, Huntingdon, Cambridgeshire PE29 6XX

A CIP catalogue record for this book is available from the British Library

ISBN 978 1 84842 840 9

Alys, Always was first performed at the Bridge Theatre, London, on 5 March 2019 (previews from 25 February). The cast was as follows:

FRANCES	Joanne Froggatt
ALYS	Joanna David
PC NAGRA	Vineeta Rishi
OLIVER	Simon Manyonda
MARY	Sylvestra Le Touzel
SID	Danny Ashok
CHARLOTTE	Joanna David
LAURENCE	Robert Glenister
POLLY	Leah Gayer
TEDDY	Sam Woolf
JULIA PRICE	Vineeta Rishi
MRS THORPE	Sue Wallace
MR THORPE	Jeff Rawle
ROBIN	Jeff Rawle
AUDREY	Sylvestra Le Touzel
CELLIST	Maddie Cutter

Director	Nicholas Hytner
Production Designer	Bob Crowley
Costume Designer	Christina Cunningham
Composer	Grant Olding
Lighting Designer	Jon Clark
Sound Designer	Gareth Fry
Video Designer	Luke Halls
Assistant Director	Cara Nolan
Associate Designer	Jaimie Todd
Associate Video Designer	Zakk Hein
Casting Director	Cara Beckinsale
Costume Supervisor	Zeb Lalljee
Props Supervisor	Lily Mollgaard
Production Manager	Kate West

For Brian Coxon (1934–2010)

– my first and favourite unreliable narrator.

Characters

FRANCES THORPE
ALYS KYTE
PC
OLIVER CULPEPPER
RECEPTIONIST, *voice only*
SID
MARY PYM
ROBIN McALFREE
CHARLOTTE BLACK
LAURENCE KYTE
POLLY KYTE
TEDDY KYTE
MRS THORPE
MR THORPE
AUDREY CULLUM
JULIA PRICE, *non-speaking*

Also POLICE OFFICERS, COURIER, WAITER

This text went to press before the end of rehearsals and so may differ slightly from the play as performed.

Chapter One

Weather – wind lashing trees along a rural B road.

The slow squeak and tock of cheap windscreen wipers clearing sleet.

FRANCES *exercises restraint as she tells us what's happening. But it isn't going to end well.*

FRANCES. It's not long after six, but it's been dark for hours…

And the roads are completely deserted.

There's sleet on the windscreen. The heat's up full blast. But it's still all steamed over.

I'm approaching the Imberly crossroads. I just touch the brake, but I feel the tyres slide – and it scares me…

A light sweeps across her for a moment.

And that's when I see the big Audi Estate – pulling up, on the Biddenbrooke road.

And I'm really relieved to see somebody else.

It's my right of way, but the Audi pulls out. I don't mind, because I'd rather follow, you know…?

But her tail lights are there for a moment, then gone.

So I'm left in the dark, on my own.

FRANCES*'s mood darkens accordingly.*

And the fog's really thick as the road winds down into Wistleborough Wood…

And I'm starting to really hate my life… I'm hating my life and my tinny red Fiat and –

A cacophony of metal and glass crashing – and then silence… FRANCES hurries to a ditch at the side of the road from which a car's tail lights glow…

Hello…?

ALYS's voice, from within – muffled, distressed.

ALYS (*offstage*). Hello…? Are you there? I can't see you… Is somebody there?

FRANCES. Yes… Are you alright? I've called for help.

ALYS (*offstage*). Oh, thank you… thank you… I thought I heard someone…

FRANCES presses her face against a window, but can see nothing.

FRANCES. Are you hurt, do you think?

ALYS (*offstage*). My… my legs aren't too good… They don't seem to be working…

FRANCES. I could try to get down to you, but I'm worried in case…

ALYS (*offstage*). No, that's probably best. Let's just wait.

FRANCES acquiesces, helpless. Silence settles between them for a moment. Then –

I think I might have knocked my head.

FRANCES. Is it bleeding?

ALYS (*offstage*). It doesn't seem to be…

FRANCES. The ambulance won't be long. I'm sure.

ALYS (*offstage*). You won't leave me…?

FRANCES. Of course not…

ALYS (*offstage*). Thank you. That's kind.

I'm being a nuisance.

FRANCES. Don't be silly. What's your name?

FRANCES *waits – no reply.*

Hello…?

FRANCES *presses her face against the glass, worried.*
Finally –

Can you hear me…?

ALYS (*offstage*). Yes… it's Alys. With a 'y'.

FRANCES *is relieved.*

FRANCES. Alys. Okay. Well, I'm Frances. With an 'e'.

ALYS (*offstage*). Ha. Mm.

ALYS *sounds weak.*

FRANCES. Listen, Alys, you're going to be fine.

ALYS (*offstage*). I thought I saw a dog in the road, you see…
A dog or a fox. Or…

A strange sound – a small cry of pain, perhaps. FRANCES
quickens, worried.

FRANCES. Alys…?

No reply.

It won't be much longer. But you need to keep talking…

Alys?

FRANCES *waits, then…*

Are you cold?

ALYS (*offstage*). I don't think so. Are you?

FRANCES. I'm fine.

FRANCES *searches for small talk.*

Have you had a nice Christmas?

ALYS (*offstage*). Not especially. No. And yourself?

FRANCES. No, not really

ALYS (*offstage*). Oh well… can't complain.

The absurdity of the exchange settles for a moment before ALYS *gives up the strange cry of pain again.* FRANCES *is frightened now.*

FRANCES. Alys… Say something…?

But then – sirens, blue flashing lights!

Oh Alys, they're here, look! They're coming, hold on!

FRANCES *waves her arms, shouts over the siren…*

Over here! Can you see me? Can you see me…?

A bright light finds FRANCES *and a* FEMALE POLICE OFFICER *races in to cloak her in a foil wrap, hurries her aside, as police colleagues work on the crashed car.* FRANCES *explains to the* PC –

It's my right of way, but the Audi pulls out.

PC. You said that before.

FRANCES. Did I?

We see now the PC *has written all this in her notepad.*

PC. It's alright, it's the shock. So, you got to the crossroads. It's your right of way. She pulls out. Would you say she was speeding?

FRANCES. No – I don't think so… Will she be alright?

PC. You've been brilliant.

FRANCES. But is Alys going to be…?

The PC *cuts her off…*

PC. Are you okay to drive on to London?

FRANCES *tries to catch up…*

Might be best to go back to your parents' place?

FRANCES. No – God, no. I… I've got work tomorrow.

PC. What is it you do?

FRANCES. A newspaper.

The PC *packs her notepad away.*

PC. Can't they manage without you for a morning?

FRANCES. Can't afford to find out. Look, I don't need this…

FRANCES *takes off the foil blanket, hands it over.*

PC. Anyone waiting at home for you?

FRANCES. I'll be fine. Honestly. Thanks.

PC. Okay. But drive safe. I'll be in touch.

The PC *leaves to join her colleagues.* FRANCES *steps away from the crash site, still very shaken.*

FRANCES *talks to us. She's exhausted, still upset.*

FRANCES. By the time I get home, Tesco Metro's long closed. Even the kebab place downstairs from me's shut. I park right outside, and just sit in the car.

I make fists to stop my hands shaking. And I think: Frances… you're not so badly off.

A fruity voice booms into FRANCES*'s world –*

OLIVER. 'Death by Desire', anyone?

The offices of The Questioner *are conjured into being.*

RECEPTIONIST'S VOICE. Good morning, *The Questioner*…? Robin McAllfree? Certainly – can I ask who's calling?

OLIVER. 'Keep Calm and Cupcake'?

RECEPTIONIST'S VOICE. Good morning, *The Questioner*? Frances Thorpe? Certainly – can I ask who's calling?

FRANCES *quickly comes to, settles at her desk, works hard, against the clock. Her colleague* OLIVER *brandishes another book, broadcasting to no one in particular.*

OLIVER. Have they ever read the paper? I mean, how often has *The Questioner*'s Books section devoted its column inches to why Frenchwomen can eat but not get fat?

Without looking up –

FRANCES. We might think about that for a tie-in with Health…

OLIVER. No!

OLIVER rejects the book, his performance a familiar irritation to his colleagues – including SID from TV and Travel, trying to work in the background. OLIVER hurls the last of the books into a blue Ikea bag. FRANCES works on.

Right – these for the review cupboard, these straight to Oxfam? Frances…?

FRANCES glances over.

FRANCES. Got it.

She looks back at the screen.

OLIVER. Now would be good.

FRANCES. Let me just…

OLIVER. Hey, it's not me. But Mary will have a kitten if she gets in and…

A woman's voice rings through the room –

MARY. Ambrose, darling, you've made me the happiest woman alive.

FRANCES. Shit.

MARY arrives, on the phone. She juggles the handset with a coffee, an Hermés handbag bulging with paperwork, and a large carrier bag from The White Company.

FRANCES races to drag the Ikea bag away with one hand, the bundle of books under the other arm. Crouches to stash the review copies in a cupboard.

MARY. Truly – I'm in bliss… I'll get it emailed across to you…

But there's some obstacle… MARY *grimaces…*

Oh…? No, no – understood – absolutely. A hard copy always so much nicer… I'll have it biked round to you now…

OLIVER *waves hello to* MARY.

So thrilled you can do this.

MARY *hangs up, exhales. Her tone changes.*

Where's Frances?

FRANCES *presents herself…*

FRANCES. Here.

MARY. Ambrose Pritchett's reviewing the new Paul Crewe. Get the book to him in Richmond? And chop chop. He leaves for Heathrow at eleven.

FRANCES *is thrown by the urgency of the request…*

FRANCES. This morning…?

MARY. Yes, of course this morning!

MARY *and* OLIVER *share a look…*

Who leaves for a plane at eleven at night?

Oh, and Frances, there's this…

She hands FRANCES *the bag from The White Company.*
FRANCES *wonders, confused… Is it for her…?*

FRANCES. The White Company. Nice.

MARY. A festive effort from Susie Smythe. You'd think she'd know better. Put it in the present cupboard, would you?

FRANCES. Sure, where's the Paul Crewe?

MARY *baffles…*

MARY. Do I look like a fucking librarian, darling?

OLIVER *smiles.* FRANCES *hurries off to look…* MARY *settles at her desk with a heavy sigh.*

OLIVER. Good Christmas?

MARY. Heavenly, thank you, Oliver. Although it already feels long gone.

FRANCES. Hi – yes, I need a bike straight away…

OLIVER. Were you in Norfolk for the whole show?

MARY. Came back for New Year at the Everetts'…

OLIVER. Oh, I love the Everetts!

FRANCES. Richmond. By eleven… Yes, I know. Thank you…

OLIVER. And have the kids gone back?

FRANCES. Yes – on this number…

> FRANCES *dedicates herself to search through the review cupboard…*

MARY. Tiggy's back up to St Andrews on Tuesday – she's got work experience at Guy's firm first. Leo's at home for another fortnight – it seems the more you pay a school, the less time they actually spend there. Thank God he's gone skiing with my sister's kids this week… How about you? Nice break?

OLIVER. Lovely… Dad's special was on on Boxing Day –

MARY. I forgot! Well, I'll catch it on iPlayer…

OLIVER. Worth a look…

> OLIVER *waits until* MARY*'s settled, then stands, pats his pockets, checking for cigarettes, lighter…*

> Mary, I'm just nipping out to feed the meter. Can I get you anything?

> MARY *reacts badly. She glances over to a glass wall, behind which* ROBIN McALLFREE *paces, talking into his Bluetooth earpiece.*

MARY. Don't people just pay for parking by phone these days?

OLIVER. Pratt Street's still old-school.

MARY. Well let Frances do it. With things as they are, you need to think what it looks like. Robin sees everything. And you're out of the office too often – all those cigarette breaks with Sasha from Fashion...

OLIVER. Point taken.

MARY*'s eyes widen in warning.*

MARY. Trust me, at times like this, what it *looks like* is everything.

FRANCES *locates the book!*

FRANCES. Got it!

Hallelujah! She searches for an envelope to pack it... Then her phone rings – she answers it – with some urgency –

Hello...? I'm just bringing it down...

The PC *appears on stage – though not in the office.*

PC. Frances? It's PC Tina Nagra...

FRANCES. Oh, I'm sorry – I thought you were somebody else.

PC. I wish! How're you getting on?

FRANCES. Well, uh... I'm busy...

She resumes packing the book, the phone trapped between shoulder and ear.

PC. I'll be quick then – just to let you know, all the evidence confirms your account of what happened. The driver tried to avoid something in the road, black ice did the rest.

FRANCES. Great. Not great, I mean, but... I'm sorry, it's just work.

PC. You sound a bit jumpy.

FRANCES. No – I'm fine.

PC. Good.

FRANCES. So if that's it...?

PC. Just one other thing... Yeah... The family would like to meet you.

FRANCES *is astonished.*

FRANCES. What?

PC. You were the last person to speak to their loved one. Would you have a problem with that?

FRANCES *considers for a grim moment.*

FRANCES. I don't think I can do that... The thing is... I just want to move on.

PC. Sometimes witnesses find it cathartic... it helps them to close the chapter...

FRANCES *grapples with the idea... Then her phone buzzes, interrupts – she's released...*

FRANCES. Sorry, I've got a call coming in... I'll give it some thought. Really sorry.

FRANCES *hangs up, picks up the other call... The* PC *is abandoned, melts away.*

Hi – yes, yes... I'm on the way down with it now...

A bike-helmeted COURIER *rushes to take the book from* FRANCES *and hurries it away.*

FRANCES *faces out –*

So I get the Paul Crewe to Ambrose Pritchett, I feed Oliver's meter, then I'm back at the desk. I have lunch in the office to cover the phones.

I work late. I don't mind.

And then I go back to the flat to sleep. But I don't sleep, of course. There are foxes out back. Singing, fighting, fucking – who knows? And if I'm honest, I've not really slept since it happened.

A voice intrudes – SID *from TV and Travel.*

SID. How do you stand it?!

SID*'s on his lunchbreak outside the office, eating a sandwich.*
FRANCES *approaches with a clutch of takeaway coffees.*

FRANCES. I'm sorry?

SID. Oliver. 'Oh yah could you feed my meter…' I'd feed a King Edward up his exhaust pipe.

FRANCES *struggles to rally.*

FRANCES. You get used to it.

SID. Parked in Pratt Street – you couldn't make it up.

FRANCES. He's a good writer though, when he bothers. Stylish.

SID. Style over substance. Hey – has Mary let anything slip – about this round of cuts?

FRANCES. Mary never lets anything slip. Why, what are they saying in TV and Travel?

SID. Nothing I'd trust.

FRANCES *is late now.*

FRANCES. Sid, I'd better get in…

SID. Get in and look useful!

FRANCES *turns on him, slightly riled.*

FRANCES. I am useful.

SID *laughs as* FRANCES *heads into the office.*

RECEPTIONIST'S VOICE. I'm sorry, Mr McAllfree's in a meeting at the moment… Thank you…

MARY *is going through her mail,* OLIVER *is sorting the latest arrival of books…* FRANCES *distributes the coffees…*

FRANCES. Flat white with almond milk.

OLIVER. Great. Thanks.

FRANCES. Your mint tea.

MARY nods, barely looks up. FRANCES settles at her desk.

OLIVER. Oh, here's something big… *Affliction*. The new Laurence Kyte…

He hands MARY a book. Her eyes widen.

MARY. You'd think they'd push back publication.

OLIVER. Maybe it's too late…

MARY. He'll be in no state to do press. Must be *devastated*.

She sits with the grim thought for a moment. Then:

Ask for an interview all the same.

OLIVER. Surely he won't want…

MARY. Of course he won't. But this is why we pay you to party with the PRs. Call the publicist. Offer them anything.

He dials. MARY keeps an ear open…

FRANCES. Sorry, Mary – Anne Maxwell still hasn't filed. Do you want me to chase her or…?

MARY. Yes. Polite nudge.

OLIVER shifts into oily charm mode…

OLIVER. Hi Sophie – yeah… how's you…?

FRANCES (*to* MARY). And are you happy for me to sign off on *The Future of Poetry*?

OLIVER. Yeah, pretty good, pretty good.

MARY (*to* FRANCES). Go ahead.

OLIVER. Great… Yeah, so, I was wondering… the new Laurence Kyte… I know, awful… I know… Ah, I knew you were going to say that – but…

FRANCES notes MARY's keen interest in the reply…
OLIVER parries a 'no'…

Really? Not even for me…?

Apparently not...

The thing is, he could totally call the shots, goes without saying... But sure, in the circs...

He makes a throat-cutting gesture for MARY*'s benefit.*
MARY *shrugs, frustrated.*

I know... terrible, terrible. Well, if he changes his mind... By the way – what actually happened...? Do you know? Oh god... God... Yeah – you too. Take care, babe. See you soon.

OLIVER *hangs up.*

MARY. Damn.

OLIVER. He's not doing any publicity. Sophie's sick as a pike about it. Should we get Berenice to review it? Or Simon?

MARY. Simon. *Damn.* Unless... do you think there's a chance we could get it to Daniel Day-Lewis?

OLIVER. To review?

MARY *shrugs.*

MARY. A bit off-piste. But he did win the Oscar for *Time's Revenge.* I know that was back in the noughties... Still, he and Kyte got pretty chummy...

OLIVER. Robin would die.

MARY. But could we press Daniel Day-Lewis to deliver Thursday week...? I mean, who's going to do that?

OLIVER *raises both hands in refusal.*

No. It'll have to be Simon. But let's do a feature we can shoehorn Kyte into... 'Booker Prize Winners – where are they now?'

OLIVER. Got it. Frances – can you get this out to Simon Ward-Johnson? The new Laurence Kyte – poor bastard.

FRANCES *takes the book. But doesn't understand –*

FRANCES. What's poor about him?

OLIVER. Christ – keep up…

MARY addresses OLIVER in an urgent whisper.

MARY. Oliver – did she say anything else…?

As they exchange gossip, FRANCES faces out with the book…

FRANCES. And then I read the dedication.

FRANCES overhears OLIVER and MARY now.

OLIVER. Apparently she lost control.

FRANCES. 'For Alys. Always.'

OLIVER. Black ice or something.

FRANCES. Alys with a 'y'.

MARY. Horrible. There but for the grace of God…

FRANCES. Go I.

FRANCES mind floods with questions…

OLIVER. Would've been a coup if we'd talked him into doing it…

FRANCES *(to herself)*. Alys Kyte.

MARY. Can you imagine?!

FRANCES considers a moment, dials a number on her phone:

FRANCES. Hello, Tina. It's Frances Thorpe. I've got myself together a bit. If you really think it would help… I'm okay to meet the family.

The office disappears.

Chapter Two

FRANCES. Two days later, I'm on the way. The Kytes' place isn't far from mine, but trust me – it's another world.

I leave behind the Poundland, the Paddy Power and Oxfam. Twenty minutes later, everything's changed. It's all organic butchers', hot yoga, posh kidswear. At Pain Quotidien, I turn off the high street...

It's not long after six, but it's already dark...

I look in through their windows – at the just-dug basement kitchens, Agas no one cooks on. All those shiny lives.

CHARLOTTE BLACK – *an older woman, warm, expansive – approaches carrying a spectacular bouquet.* FRANCES *is in the Kyte family home.*

CHARLOTTE. Charlotte Black. Friend of the family. Do come in... Can you believe all these flowers? Even this long after the funeral, they just keep arriving. The outpouring's extraordinary. There are no vases left, we've had to use ice buckets, fill all the sinks... The tuberose are actually making me giddy.

She dumps the bouquet in a bucket.

Come through...

FRANCES *eyes dart about as* CHARLOTTE *leads the way –*

LAURENCE *enters. He and* FRANCES *brace, then –*

LAURENCE. Laurence Kyte. May I call you Frances?

FRANCES. Yes, of course...

He takes her hand. Holds on to it. Eventually –

LAURENCE. Thanks for agreeing to see us. Really.

FRANCES *searches for the right words. But –*

FRANCES. I'm so very sorry for your loss.

The loss seems to hit LAURENCE *afresh. A fragile-looking young woman arrives –* POLLY.

POLLY. Daddy…?

The spell is broken – LAURENCE *releases* FRANCES *and embraces* POLLY. *A young man appears too –* TEDDY. *He hangs back.*

LAURENCE. These are my children, Edward and Polly. And you've met Charlotte – my dear friend. And agent. Let's all sit down, shall we?

CHARLOTTE. I'll put the kettle on. Tea or coffee, Frances?

Before FRANCES *can answer…*

LAURENCE. Oh, Charlotte – I think this calls for a drink.

CHARLOTTE *allows this. He heads off to fetch a bottle, leaving* FRANCES *behind with the others.*

CHARLOTTE. Please, do sit…

She ushers FRANCES *to a chair. They sit in silence for a moment, until* TEDDY *steps up – speaks to* FRANCES. *He doesn't find it easy.*

TEDDY. So, Tina, the police liaison, was saying you live nearby?

FRANCES. Yes – just down the hill.

CHARLOTTE *perks up –*

CHARLOTTE. Those pretty streets near Planet Organic?

FRANCES. A little bit further.

The table sinks back into silence until LAURENCE *returns with a bottle of wine, glugs it into glasses.*

CHARLOTTE. No – thank you, Laurence.

CHARLOTTE *declines.* FRANCES *politely accepts.* LAURENCE *turns to* FRANCES, *the bottle hovering over her glass.*

LAURENCE. And…

He blanks her name. TEDDY *prompts him, irritable.*

TEDDY. 'Frances.'

LAURENCE. Frances – forgive me… I'm really not firing
on all…

FRANCES. Thank you.

He pours wine for her, the others. Sits.

LAURENCE. Well, we… we wanted to tell you how grateful
we are. We've been walked through your statement, the gist
of it, at least, and… it's… it's been a comfort.

LAURENCE *stutters, stalls…* POLLY *covers her mouth.*
TEDDY *pipes up…*

TEDDY. We're very grateful Mum wasn't on her own at the
end. So thankful you pulled in, stayed with her… You tried.

FRANCES *nods. The hopelessness of it all sits between
them, until:*

POLLY. Can you tell us what she said…? I mean I know it's in
the file… but… I couldn't bear to read it. None of us could.

FRANCES *nods, understanding.*

Did she sound *like herself*?

CHARLOTTE. Polly, I'm not sure that Frances is in a position
to answer that…

FRANCES. That's fine. I'll tell you what I can.

FRANCES *composes herself for a moment, then:*

I didn't know Alys before. Of course. But… we talked, a
little. She was quite… lucid, together… if that's what you're
asking? She wasn't in distress, or at least if she was, she
controlled it. You do know I couldn't see her?

FRANCES *glances around the table. The others are hanging
on every word. The heat of their attention lights her up.*

It was very dark… and with that and the position of the car…

FRANCES *shrugs*.

Alys told me she might have hit her head, and that her legs were injured, but she didn't seem to be in pain. She said she'd come off the road avoiding a dog, or a fox.

POLLY *makes a noise: part-laugh, part-sob.* CHARLOTTE *catches hold of her hand.*

She thanked me for keeping her company. I remember thinking, what a dignified sort of person she seemed. In fact at one point she apologised…

LAURENCE. Christ.

LAURENCE *suddenly bows his head, affected.* FRANCES *allows a moment then presses on.*

FRANCES. She was worried she'd been a nuisance.

They absorb this.

I'm afraid that's more or less it.

The whole table is in a terrible state of suspension…

POLLY. That's everything.

FRANCES *nods. It's simply not enough… not the closure they had hoped for.*

FRANCES. I'm afraid so.

POLLY. God…

Their faces hang, desolate. The grief goes on and on…

A beat of indecision, then –

FRANCES. Except, of course…

Their faces lift…

…right at the end… when I told her I could see the ambulance – 'Tell them I love them.'

LAURENCE *trembles as* FRANCES *holds him in her gaze –*

She said 'Tell them I love them.' There was nothing after that.

LAURENCE *sighs heavily, seems to fold in on himself.*
POLLY *reaches out and grips* FRANCES*'s hand.*
FRANCES *is surprised, but responds kindly.* CHARLOTTE
covers her mouth. TEDDY *stares at the table. The only
sound is* POLLY, *weeping, until she finally manages –*

POLLY. *Thank* you.

FRANCES. I just wish I could have done more.

LAURENCE *fights to gather himself.*

LAURENCE. Yes... You've been very kind, Frances. Does anyone else want to ask anything?

A silence around the table.

Well then...

They sit in the aftermath. Until –

FRANCES. I probably ought to...

CHARLOTTE. I'll see Frances out.

But TEDDY *interrupts – addresses* FRANCES.

TEDDY. What were you doing out on that road?

FRANCES. My parents retired to Frynborough. I'd been staying with them.

TEDDY. I see.

FRANCES *ventures, carefully –*

FRANCES. What was Alys doing there?

TEDDY. We've got a place in Biddenbrooke.

FRANCES *knows the village.*

FRANCES. Ah, really...?

TEDDY. That's where we'd all been for Christmas.

TEDDY*'s tone is slightly chilly.*

LAURENCE. The children and I were staying on. But Alys...
Alys needed to get back to London. There was a blind woman she used to read to. Didn't want to let her down.

POLLY. That's what she was like. Always putting other people first.

FRANCES *takes this all in.*

FRANCES. Oh dear... I wish I could have known her. I don't know what else I can say... So...

FRANCES *is on the edge of leaving.* POLLY *can't bear it...*

POLLY. Oh, but don't go... Won't you finish your glass?

FRANCES. That's kind, but...

But POLLY *grabs* FRANCES*'s arm –*

POLLY. Stay for supper?

LAURENCE. Polly, it's alright...

FRANCES *tries to take control.*

POLLY. I don't want you to just leave, and then... that's *it...*

FRANCES *glances at* LAURENCE.

FRANCES. You can always get in touch if you want to.

POLLY. Through the police?! That's just horrible...

TEDDY. Pol...

POLLY. I don't want to lose her... Not yet...

FRANCES. It's fine – I'll give you my number.

POLLY *seizes on this.*

POLLY. Will you? Thank you, Frances...

She takes out her phone, hand shaking...

CHARLOTTE. Polly dear...

POLLY*'s crying now...*

POLLY. I can't do it... I can't even see...

FRANCES. Here – give me your phone...

She takes POLLY*'s phone. Dials her own number. A vibrating sound from* FRANCES*'s coat pocket... Talks to* POLLY, *as though she were a child.*

FRANCES. There. You've got me now.

POLLY. Thank you.

FRANCES *hands back the phone.* POLLY *turns to the others.*

She should come to the memorial.

TEDDY. Christ, Polly, stop.

LAURENCE. No, she's right. If you'd like to. It's not till next month – we're just about to send these out.

He hands her an invitation, a photo of ALYS *on the front.* FRANCES *studies it for a moment…*

FRANCES. This is Alys.

LAURENCE. Yes.

TEDDY *gets up abruptly, leaves the room.* LAURENCE *nods, can hardly bear the thought of it.* POLLY *gets up and embraces* FRANCES.

POLLY. Thank you, Frances – you can't know what this means.

FRANCES *delicately detaches herself from* POLLY.

FRANCES. I'm glad to have met you, Polly.

CHARLOTTE. Shall we…?

CHARLOTTE *escorts her away, back through the floral tributes.* LAURENCE *leads* POLLY *off.*

Goodness, that was terrible. For you too, I'm quite sure. She's so dreadfully missed.

CHARLOTTE *struggles with emotion, overwhelmed for a moment. Then –*

All these flowers! Alys loved flowers. You know about her garden at Biddenbrooke?

FRANCES. No…

CHARLOTTE. Oh, it's quite famous. All white, of course. God, that garden! Who will look after it now?

CHARLOTTE *seizes on an idea –*

Here –

She grabs a huge bouquet… holds it out to FRANCES.

FRANCES. I couldn't…

CHARLOTTE. For heaven's sake! She'd have hated them to just sit there in a dark room.

CHARLOTTE *reads the card on the flowers.*

From the Controller of Radio 4. No one will even miss them…

FRANCES. Thank you.

CHARLOTTE. You were a part of this too. I hope you can put it behind you now.

The notion hangs between them for a moment.

I ought to start dinner… None of them are really eating…

FRANCES. Of course.

CHARLOTTE *takes in* FRANCES*'s face, perhaps for the last time, then –*

CHARLOTTE. Goodbye, Frances. And thank you.

CHARLOTTE *goes, leaving* FRANCES *nursing the flowers like a baby.* FRANCES *looks out.*

FRANCES. I learn some important things from my visit to the Kytes. Not least of which is that the customers at Pain Quotidien look at you very differently when you're carrying a two-hundred-pound bouquet.

She sets them down. Drinks in their loveliness.

And, of course, I learn more about Alys…

CHARLOTTE *struggles with her composure, standing at a small podium –*

CHARLOTTE. The miracle that was Alys arrived in my life quite unexpectedly when Laurence rushed into the office and gave a feverish account of his new inamorata. I'm afraid that I thought her some ghastly Lorelei, come to distract my most promising client...

Indulgent laughter from the crowd.

FRANCES. I try the flowers in various locations around the flat. Every corner is transformed by them. As if Alys had waved a wand.

CHARLOTTE. But I was quite wrong. With Alys at his side, Laurence wrote as never before.

FRANCES. I feel like a slightly different person. I'm happier at work, knowing I've these to come home to.

CHARLOTTE. Only just out of art school, she supported him – making jewellery out of salvaged junk to dazzle the buyers at Harvey Nicks. Transforming the cheapest ingredients into an absolute feast.

FRANCES. I keep the heat turned down to make them last longer – and a few still cling on when the memorial comes around.

CHARLOTTE. When the children came along, Alys threw herself into homemaking. She baked apple pies we ate there, in the orchard. Right under the trees where she'd grown the fruit. We drank great jugs of her elderflower cordial sprigged with the mint from the pots at her door. And, of course, there was her famous garden...

She stalls momentarily, throat tightening...

FRANCES. Looking around the teary crowd, I see a lot of famous faces. A few MPs... there's Melvyn Bragg, two broadsheet editors and the one from Monty Python whose name no one remembers. If a bomb dropped now, the Garrick Club would go out of business.

She pays attention now, listening to:

CHARLOTTE. Alys transfigured everything she touched. We are all so blessed to have known her. I hope that is some consolation to those who will miss her most terribly... Laurence, Teddy, Polly – our hearts go out to you.

A long look at LAURENCE... TEDDY *and* POLLY *lower their faces.*

FRANCES. Outside, afterwards, the clouds have turned to drizzle... The crowd queues to pay its respects to the family. Everyone but an elegant woman who rushes away, looking upset. She trails a thin silk scarf with blue and white stripes...

It reminds me of police tape.

A flutter of striped silk. FRANCES *watches the striped scarf disappear.*

That's when I spot Mary. And – more importantly – Mary spots me...

MARY *looks surprised, makes to approach* FRANCES, *but* –

POLLY. Frances...

FRANCES. Polly...

POLLY *hurries to bring her huge Liberty-print umbrella over* FRANCES*'s head. Cocoons the two of them inside it.*

POLLY. Oh, I hoped I'd see you. I've almost called you so many times.

FRANCES. You should have...

POLLY. No I shouldn't.

POLLY *grips her arm.*

Come around the side, will you? I can't stand all these people... I don't even know half of them...

FRANCES *goes, willingly... Once they're alone,* POLLY *tries to juggle the umbrella and her cigarette and lighter.*

FRANCES. Here – give that to me.

POLLY. Mum would have hated this. She loathed crowds, big parties.

POLLY *hands off the umbrella, lights her cigarette, takes a deep drag. Exhales.*

That's better.

FRANCES. How are you?

> POLLY *shakes her head, shrugs, letting* FRANCES *hold the umbrella over them.*

POLLY. Do you really want to know?

FRANCES. Of course.

POLLY. Because mostly people don't.

FRANCES. Polly…

> FRANCES *looks at her, waits…* POLLY *yields to the steady attention.*

POLLY. Some mornings I wake up, and I've actually forgotten… And then I remember.

FRANCES. Oh, sweetheart…

> *She rests her hand on* POLLY*'s arm.*

POLLY. I think about her all the time. Things I wish I could tell her or ask her. And then all this shit at college…

> *Before* FRANCES *can pursue this,* MARY *arrives.*

MARY. Frances…? What a surprise…?

> POLLY *startles, bolts.*

POLLY. Sorry, Frances. I'll give you a call.

> *And she's gone, to join* TEDDY, *leaving* FRANCES *holding the umbrella.*

MARY. Oh, I do apologise, I didn't mean to…

FRANCES. That's alright…

MARY. Was that Polly Kyte…?

FRANCES. I'd better check on her…

MARY. Of course…

> FRANCES *escapes from* MARY *and almost immediately encounters –*

FRANCES. Laurence…

LAURENCE. Ah…

He looks blank – FRANCES *prompts him.*

FRANCES. Frances.

LAURENCE. God, of course. Sorry – I'm a bit of a wreck…

FRANCES. Please – don't apologise.

LAURENCE. Good of you to come.

Some distance away, MARY *watches closely…* FRANCES *uses the umbrella to conceal and reveal the encounter as it suits her.*

FRANCES. Let me get this…

She brushes the arm of his jacket.

It's just pollen – you must have brushed against the flowers.

LAURENCE. Oh…?

He examines his jacket – quite clean.

FRANCES. All fine now. Well, I just wanted to make sure I spoke to you, to say how touched I was.

And FRANCES *leans forward and kisses him on the cheek.* LAURENCE *seems somewhat surprised.*

Take care.

LAURENCE *nods, nonplussed, moves off.*

And as I leave – still carrying Polly's beautiful Liberty-print umbrella – I wave to Teddy in the distance.

TEDDY *blanks her, hating everyone.*

TEDDY (*to* POLLY). What a fucking show. If you put this on Facebook, I'll kill you.

POLLY. Teddy…

TEDDY *heads off,* POLLY *trailing behind him.*

FRANCES. He doesn't seem to see me. But that doesn't matter, because Mary does.

Chapter Three

MARY *arrives in the office – on the phone, as usual, but juggling two coffees today.*

MARY (*into her phone*). Oh, file when you're ready, darling. Any time on Thursday will be fine.

RECEPTIONIST'S VOICE. Good morning, *The Questioner*? Sasha Sykes? Certainly – can I ask who's calling?

She arrives at her desk, drops her bag, and turns to FRANCES.

MARY. Latte or flat white?

FRANCES. I'm sorry?

MARY. I really don't mind. You choose.

FRANCES *is confused…* MARY *beams a smile.*

FRANCES. Flat white.

MARY. Perfect.

She hands FRANCES *the cup, tears open a bag containing two croissants.*

I'm supposed to be on decaf. Robin's targets and tractions are giving me an ulcer. Hey-ho.

FRANCES. Right.

FRANCES *tentatively returns to work.*

MARY. Little pastry?

FRANCES *looks up, takes one out of politeness.*

I didn't know you knew the Kytes? Unbelievably sad.

FRANCES. Yes, it is.

MARY. I mean, *really.*

MARY *waits, greedy…*

FRANCES. Poor Laurence seems lost. Don't you think? But then, they all do…

MARY. Well, I hardly know them. The invitation to the memorial came from the publishers. I never met Alys.

MARY *waits again… then…*

FRANCES. Alys wasn't keen on crowds and parties. Always happiest in her garden at Biddenbrooke.

MARY *is mesmerised.*

Anyway, thanks for this…

FRANCES *takes a sip of her coffee. Gets back to work.* MARY *considers, then…*

MARY. The new Sunil Ranjan. Does it interest you?

FRANCES *looks up.*

FRANCES. I've read his others. Loved them both…

MARY. Good. Six hundred words, a week on Thursday?

FRANCES. A review?

MARY. I was going to let Oliver do it, but –

She passes FRANCES *the weighty tome.*

FRANCES. Thank you…

MARY. If he can't even make it in on time…

FRANCES. He covered the Ariana Grande biog launch last night.

MARY. And partied hard afterwards by the looks of the Instagram feed.

FRANCES. Sorry – I don't Instagram.

MARY. Of course you don't. I have no choice – Robin's obsessed with it. But he's not so impressed today. Countless snaps of Oliver Culpepper coked off his tits, messing about with a helium canister!

MARY *throws up her hands.*

FRANCES. I'm happy to look into the social-media side. If that's a help? There are some interesting new platforms we might look at for teasers to premium content and so on. But I'm not interested in... you know...? Being the story.

MARY *slumps with relief.*

MARY. Frances... *Thank* you. Could you pop all that in an email to me?

FRANCES. Of course.

MARY. Plans for Easter...?

FRANCES. Just a visit to my parents' place. Suffolk. I'll take this along.

MARY. Fabulous.

She sets down the Sunil Ranjan. MARY *winks conspiratorially before wheeling away with her latte, heading for* ROBIN*'s office.*

FRANCES. Sunil Ranjan sits in the passenger seat, as I drive back – for the first time since Alys. I'm a little apprehensive at first, to be honest. But I've downloaded three hours of *Gardeners' Question Time.* A new interest. So the journey flies by.

MRS THORPE*'s voice rings out ahead of her... She appears only for a moment, wearing an apron.*

MRS THORPE. Your room's all ready!

She disappears again. FRANCES *faces out.*

FRANCES. I don't have to see it to know what that means. Three padded coat hangers, fanned out on the bed. A bath towel, a flannel and a guest soap.

MRS THORPE *returns with two mugs of tea. Hands one to* FRANCES.

MRS THORPE. How's London? Busy, is it?

FRANCES. Pretty busy.

MRS THORPE. We had the Pearsons visit last weekend. Their Clare lives quite near you...?

FRANCES. Acton's not near me.

MRS THORPE. Do you see her...?

FRANCES. Clare Pearson?

MRS THORPE *waits, all curiosity. A bald lie –*

I thought I saw her going into Selfridges last week. But she was quite far away, I couldn't be sure.

MRS THORPE *is delighted.*

MRS THORPE. She's made friends with your sister on LinkedIn.

MR THORPE *arrives.*

MR THORPE. I took your bag up.

FRANCES. Thanks.

MRS THORPE. Are you on LinkedIn? Hester swears by it.

FRANCES. Hester works for EE. It's different.

MR THORPE. Been headhunted by Vodaphone. But they want her to go to Hamburg. Why would Hester go to Hamburg? She's got what she wants right here – lovely kids in a good school, four bedrooms – two en suite – in a very nice part of London.

FRANCES. I think Croydon's actually in Surrey.

MRS THORPE. You went round for dinner last weekend.

FRANCES. Pizza. They popped out. I babysat.

MR THORPE. Hester says you like to watch their big TV.

FRANCES. Does she.

The mood flattens.

Well, I might try to pull in a little bit of work. I'm reviewing the new Sunil Ranjan...

MRS THORPE *is impressed but...*

MR THORPE. I wish I had the time to read. I don't know when people fit it in.

He goes off. A moment, then…

MRS THORPE. I love my Judy Arbuthnots. They're not literature. You couldn't call them that.

FRANCES. As long as you enjoy them…

MRS THORPE. I like a happy ending.

MRS THORPE *struggles for a moment, anxious to explain herself…*

When you open a book, it's like opening a door to another world… A nicer one.

MRS THORPE*'s life seems to brighten, but –*

Sometimes, at the end… I feel so sad…

MRS THORPE *fills with genuine emotion.*

I don't want to leave.

A long moment between FRANCES *and her mother.* FRANCES *knows exactly how she feels.* FRANCES *looks out front.*

FRANCES. That's when I decide to call Polly.

Chapter Four

POLLY *and* FRANCES *meet at The Wolseley.*

POLLY. Frances!

FRANCES. Oh – before I forget…

> FRANCES *hands over* POLLY*'s umbrella.*

POLLY. You shouldn't have. I don't even know whose it is –
someone left it at the house aeons ago.

FRANCES. Ah.

POLLY. Is this place okay? A bit bougie, but I like it. Dad
always comes here. They've given us his table!

> FRANCES *laughs.*

FRANCES. Have they?

POLLY. I got Charlotte to book it. We turned up without a
booking once and Bill Nighy was sitting at it. Dad went
batshit. It's one of the best ones – everyone can see you.
Dad always says – never mind your ranking on Amazon,
you can tell how the books are doing from where they seat
you at The Wolseley.

FRANCES. That's very funny.

POLLY. He used to love The Ivy, but there's always paparazzi
outside now. It's great you could take some time off…

FRANCES. I work at a Sunday newspaper.

> POLLY *doesn't like this news.*

POLLY. Oh…?

FRANCES. *The Questioner.* We work late Thursday nights,
getting the Arts pages off to the printer. So Fridays are
easier days.

POLLY. Right. Look, I know it sounds silly, but this is all in
confidence when we talk?

FRANCES. Of course.

POLLY. You wouldn't write about it?

FRANCES. I'm not that sort of journalist. I'm a sub-editor. I mostly check other people's spelling, move their punctuation around.

POLLY. You're not famous – for sure. I tried to look you up, but you don't exist.

FRANCES *laughs*.

I'm sorry… I didn't mean to stalk you. It's just Daddy's 'Laurence Kyte', you know?

FRANCES. Is that how it feels?

POLLY. A bit. You never know what people are after.

POLLY *shrugs*.

I wouldn't mind being a journalist. It must be fun – long boozy lunches. I hear the freebies are pretty good.

FRANCES. It's not really like that now. I wouldn't recommend it anyway – by the time you're my age, newspapers likely won't exist. The internet's wiping us out.

POLLY. Harsh. Well, like I say, I'm glad you called. It's all pretty horrid at home at the moment.

FRANCES. Polly, has something happened?

POLLY. Not exactly. I mean Dad's not in a great place… He's pretty low. And he's not writing which always makes him super-cranky.

POLLY *exhales*.

Basically, he's livid cos I've had it with drama school.

FRANCES. You're at drama school?

POLLY. I've hardly been in for a full week since Mum died! But Dad's like – 'You don't just drop out like that, think of the people who'd kill to get in there…'

FRANCES. He does have a point.

POLLY. It was like, my total dream. But once you are in, you realise it's just a load of old rubbish being churned out by these total losers. And I'm not 'dropping out'. I've got a plan.

FRANCES. Oh?

POLLY. I've got these mates – they're amazing – and we want to take a play – Shakespeare, maybe a couple of Shakespeares – on tour around the country.

FRANCES. I see.

POLLY. Just rock up and do *Love's Labour's Lost* or whatever in Scout huts and state schools. Theo – that's the director – is really committed to taking it into places which ordinarily wouldn't be exposed to proper, you know, art. It could be amazing...

FRANCES. Mm. But your father doesn't see it that way?

POLLY. He's just so fucking negative. And he doesn't understand me. Mum understood.

A moment of loss sits between them.

FRANCES. Polly, I don't know much about you and your family. But I'm pretty sure your father just wants the best for you.

POLLY*'s anger sighs away.* FRANCES *smiles.*

POLLY. What do you think I should do?

FRANCES. What would your mother have told you to do?

POLLY *thinks.*

POLLY. To give college another chance, I expect. But – then she'd have seen how miserable it was making me, and she'd have given in.

FRANCES. Well, my advice would be to tell your dad you're thinking it over. It's a tough time for all of you. A time to be pulling together – not pulling apart.

POLLY *exhales heavily.*

POLLY. You're a good listener, aren't you, Frances?

POLLY *gathers her things.*

FRANCES. Am I?

POLLY. You know when a dog listens? It really, really listens...? People usually just pile in and talk about themselves. You don't do that.

POLLY*'s attempt at a compliment sits between them for a moment. Then –*

FRANCES. Well, I ought to get back to work.

POLLY. Oh – yeah – me too. Not work, but... you know.

FRANCES. I'm always here if you want to talk. Keep me posted on how it goes.

POLLY *kisses* FRANCES *and sweeps out, crossing with the* WAITER *who presents* FRANCES *with the bill. An unpleasant surprise, but then –*

OLIVER. What's this, Frances?!

OLIVER *strides in, fuming. We're back in the office. He brandishes Sunday's paper at* FRANCES, *folded back to the Books section.*

FRANCES. Your review of the new Joanna Coffey.

OLIVER. Look closer.

MARY *glances up from a phone call, irritated, as he physically pushes the paper onto* FRANCES.

MARY (*into her phone*). No, darling, that's marvellous.

As FRANCES *understands...*

FRANCES. Shit.

MARY. Lifesaver. Bye...

MARY *finishes her call. Other people in the office are looking over now...* SID *keeps a keen eye on developments.*

OLIVER. I mean, fuck's sake!

MARY. Oliver, sit down…

FRANCES. No, he's right, Mary, a typo slipped through…

OLIVER. All you're really here for is to see I don't look stupid.

But MARY*'s incandescent.*

MARY. I said *sit*!

OLIVER *sits, resentful.* ROBIN *and the rest of the office look on.* MARY*'s voice is low, but loaded. A performance is required.*

This is a twenty-first-century workplace. Did you not see Robin's anti-bullying memo?

OLIVER. You mean his ode to the tyranny of the weak?

MARY *rounds on him, furious…*

MARY. There's nothing weak about Frances. And kindly remember she isn't here to nanny sloppy divas. We have plenty of contributors who make that kind of demand on her time. Perhaps you could save us all some trouble by checking your own copy.

OLIVER *is properly stung. He is also aware of an audience now. Reluctantly:*

OLIVER. Point taken.

OLIVER *recalibrates, considering…*

My mistake, Frances. Won't happen again.

FRANCES *glances over to TV and Travel –* SID *is punching the air in triumph. Now he's miming drinking from a glass, he taps his watch… Will* FRANCES *go for a drink later?*

MARY. Oh, and Frances. I read your piece. Very nice.

FRANCES *nods, grateful, keeps her head down.*

Music comes up – we're in the pub. SID *brings a pint for himself and a wine for* FRANCES*, still thrilled with* OLIVER*'s bollocking.*

SID. You've got another big review in this week.

FRANCES. Because I don't cost anything. Saves paying a freelancer. Cheers, Sid.

They drink.

SID. I reckon you'll be alright in the reshuffle.

FRANCES. We're such a small department – it's me or Oliver on the way out.

SID. Anything I can do to make sure it's him... say the word.

FRANCES *smiles, grateful for the support.*

FRANCES. You should be safe in TV and Travel, right?

SID. I hope so. I wouldn't want to be at the paper forever, but a couple more years would be good.

FRANCES. Then what?

SID. Oh, you know...

SID *shrugs, slightly shy...*

FRANCES. I don't, actually...

SID. It's nothing...

But she smiles at him, encouraging...

Well, the thing is, I'm writing a screenplay.

FRANCES. Amazing.

SID. Look, I know what that sounds like... But you heard about Parvaneh, didn't you?

FRANCES. Tall girl, used to be on Health and Fitness?

SID. No one thought she had anything about her. But she won this writing competition at some little theatre.

FRANCES. She wrote a play?

SID. Last I heard Spielberg had optioned it. Keira Knightley wants in. Unbelievable.

FRANCES. Wow.

SID. So, the way I see it is – someone's got to be successful… why not me?

FRANCES hears this – it chimes with her.

FRANCES. That is so true.

She hands back the glass.

Thanks for the drink.

SID. Yeah, few of us are going for a curry if you…?

FRANCES. Sorry, I've got a lot of reading…

She heaves a heavy bag over her shoulder.

SID. Blimey, that is a lot of reading.

He leans in to kiss her cheek, but FRANCES deftly blocks him with the bag…

FRANCES. See you Monday. And honestly – I'm *really* impressed.

He peels off, awkward but pleased with himself. FRANCES faces out.

Sid's right – the bag's heavy. The collected works of Laurence Kyte and some coffee-table books about famous gardens lifted from the review cupboard. I'm starting to regret bringing them all home at once when the phone beeps – a missed call.

POLLY (*voice-over*). Frances, where are you? It's all going wrong. I really need to talk to you. Just ring me when you get this. Where are you?

POLLY staggers on – drunk, dishevelled.

I'm locked out of the flat in Fulham, and my flatmate's away. And I don't want to go round to Dad's house… not like this. I am sorry.

FRANCES is calm, slightly strict, getting the measure of her.

FRANCES. That's alright. Come on in.

FRANCES *puts down her bag of books, slightly nervous of* POLLY *observing the contents.*

POLLY. Would you mind if I had a smoke?

FRANCES. I would, actually.

POLLY *puts her cigs away, chastened.*

Do you want a glass of water or a cup of tea?

POLLY. I'd really like a glass of wine. Or a beer. I don't suppose you've got a beer?

FRANCES. No.

POLLY. Fuck, I want another drink. Just one. Shit night. You know…

FRANCES *folds her arms.* POLLY *resigns herself.*

No, you're right… glass of water would be good. Still or sparkling, I don't mind.

FRANCES. Tap?

POLLY. Tap's fine. Thanks, Frances.

FRANCES *goes to get water.* POLLY *checks out* FRANCES*'s bookshelves. She calls:*

You've passed the test.

FRANCES. What test?

POLLY. Your bookshelves. No Laurence Kytes.

FRANCES *hands her a glass of water.*

FRANCES. Drink that up. I'll get some blankets and we can make up the sofa.

POLLY. Do you live on your own?

FRANCES. At the moment.

FRANCES *fetches a pillow and blanket.*

POLLY. Above a kebab shop! Keeping it real.

FRANCES. It's not Fulham, for sure.

POLLY *hears the slight reprove.*

POLLY. Oh Frances – I've ruined your night…

FRANCES. It's fine, Polly.

POLLY. I'm sorry… I just…

POLLY *covers her face, upset.* FRANCES *is losing patience.*

FRANCES. What is it?

POLLY. Laurence Kyte's being a total shit. He got together with Theo's dad and they say they'll cut off our allowances if we drop out. Theo thinks it's all my fault.

FRANCES *absorbs the non-event of it all, grabs a blanket, a pillow.*

We just had the worst row. And I'd already had a real ding-dong with Teddy…

FRANCES. With Teddy?

POLLY. Yeah, about Mum and Dad…

FRANCES *quickly registers this.*

FRANCES. What about your mum and dad…?

POLLY *stops herself, deliberates, then –*

POLLY. I almost told you before, at The Wolseley. But I just sort of bottled. But I've got to tell someone. And Teddy doesn't want to hear.

FRANCES. Hear…?

POLLY. What happened. On the day of Mum's accident.

FRANCES *takes in* POLLY's *tear-streaked face. A moment, then –*

FRANCES. Wait a minute. I've just remembered something.

FRANCES *swiftly produces two glasses and a bottle of brandy. Pours large measures.*

POLLY. Nice one… I don't drink brandy very often. Dad's a whisky man.

FRANCES. I forgot all about it. Only keep it in for cooking.

POLLY *tucks her legs up on the sofa.* FRANCES *joins her and they drink.*

Why don't you start at the beginning?

POLLY *takes a deep breath, tells her story…*

POLLY. Well, Christmas was weird. There'd been like this real atmosphere. Then, on the twenty-seventh, Mum gave Charlotte a lift to the station.

FRANCES. Charlotte was with you…?

POLLY. She always is at Christmas. And when Mum got back, she was… I don't know… different. I was making a cup of tea. I'd broken a bit off her walnut cake and she really snapped at me – said it wouldn't hurt to use a knife. That wasn't like her.

FRANCES *listens with great attentiveness.*

I took the tea back to my room – I had a script to learn. Then I heard Dad shouting. Someone had sent him this Agatha Christie first edition for Christmas.

FRANCES. An Agatha Christie?

POLLY. I know. Random. *Rebecca.*

FRANCES. *Rebecca*'s by Daphne du Maurier.

POLLY *snaps a little.*

POLLY. Is that really important?

FRANCES. No. No, of course not.

POLLY. Well he'd actually winged it across the hall. I saw it later. Broke the spine. I mean, Dad's religious about books, taking care of them, you know?

Then I heard Mum's voice from the study, really steely:

'You can change the dedication while you're at it,' she was saying.

'"Alys, Always"? It's not a tribute, it's an insult.'

I got up and saw Teddy looking over the banisters. I asked him what was going on? 'Just some bullshit,' he said.

And then Mum shouted: 'I'm sick of it. Sick of everything.' And the door slammed. That was it – she was gone. In that terrible weather. She didn't even say goodbye.

The room falls silent.

Now can you understand… why it was so important, what you told us? That she'd said she loved us.

POLLY *struggles to stem tears.* FRANCES *turns the information in her mind.*

FRANCES. Did you ever ask your father what they'd argued about?

POLLY. How could I? And I wanted to remember them happy. But I think this is why Dad's in such a shit state. I think he feels guilty. But I don't know why.

FRANCES *thinks it through… Is gentle in response.*

FRANCES. Listen, Polly, I don't think this row sounds too serious. It just seems that way to you because of what happened. Of course he feels guilty – they argued and she left, but Laurence couldn't help what happened next. Any more than you could. And your dad… he's just trying to take care of you.

POLLY. It's not working.

FRANCES. So make it easier for him. Ask for his help – with something simple. Call him in the morning and get him to pick you up from here, take you to breakfast. I bet he'd be thrilled.

POLLY. No, he's mental over this crap about college.

FRANCES. Don't worry about that. We'll soon get him back onside. Yes?

POLLY *nods, soothed a little.*

Do you think you'll be able to sleep now?

POLLY. I ought to after the brandy.

She sets down her brandy glass. FRANCES *suddenly hugs her. A proper embrace.* POLLY *responds, grateful.* FRANCES *gets up, tucks* POLLY *in, babying her.*

Frances?

FRANCES. Mm?

POLLY. Can you leave the light on? I'm not very good in the dark.

FRANCES *acknowledges the genuinely vulnerable request.* POLLY *hunkers down.* FRANCES *watches over her for a moment. Turns to us, speaking quietly, conscious of her sleeping guest...*

FRANCES. Next morning, when Polly's in the bathroom using all the hot water, I take a look through her handbag. It's a Mulberry, left open on the floor.

FRANCES *swipes a lipstick over her lips.*

Lipstick – a good one... Chantecaille... perhaps a bit too pink for me.

She pockets the lipstick.

And some brow mascara.

She swipes the brush across her brows.

I've never tried brow mascara before. But I like it. It makes me look more like myself somehow.

She pockets that too. We see POLLY *get up and stumble out, taking the pillow and blanket.*

Polly won't miss these things. And if she does, she'll think she lost them when the Moscow mules kicked in.

When Laurence drives round to collect her, I stay upstairs.
I keep the room dark, and peep down. He looks back at the
flat, at the window.

He can't see me. But I see him.

There's a new steeliness to FRANCES *now.*

At work the following month – Oliver does something
exceptionally dim.

Chapter Five

In the office – OLIVER *hands* FRANCES *a takeaway coffee.*

OLIVER. It's tempting… So tempting…

FRANCES. You should go.

OLIVER. I'm not sure.

FRANCES. Really?

OLIVER. Have you seen the latest HR memo?

FRANCES. I try not to pay too much attention.

OLIVER. You can afford to. You're invisible. Invisible people
survive. I'm a tall poppy.

FRANCES *resists the bait.*

FRANCES. If you take the Travel freebie to Italy you'll be
invisible too. For a few days, at least.

OLIVER. Be quite hard work – Sid wants two thousand words.

FRANCES. Oh, come on. 'In the Footsteps of *The Talented Mr
Ripley*…' Two nights in the Royal Hotel in San Remo…?

SID *arrives.*

SID. Including full use of the spa… If you don't want this,
there're plenty who will.

OLIVER *narrows his eyes*.

Look at Frances, gagging for it.

OLIVER. You did 'In the Footsteps of *Jane Eyre*'.

FRANCES. A day return to Keighley?

OLIVER *smirks*.

I'm guessing you turned that down.

OLIVER. I think my actual words were: 'I'd rather shit in my hands and clap.'

FRANCES. But the Amalfi Coast... At this time of year...

SID. Yes or no, Oliver...

A moment's pause as OLIVER *considers...*

OLIVER. I'm going! Sorry... poor Frances. Our in-house Cinderella.

OLIVER *hurries off, pleased with himself*. FRANCES *and* SID *high-five and head back to their desks*. MARY *hurries in*.

MARY. Any word from Ambrose Pritchett?

FRANCES. No, sorry. Nothing.

MARY. He's avoiding me. I must have left a dozen messages! If we don't have the copy tomorrow by five, we're absolutely sunk. We can't *not* review the Sturges Hardcastle. Lifestyle's got a spread about his shepherd's hut. You've read the book, haven't you?

FRANCES. It's terrific.

MARY. I hate to ask, but... by five tomorrow?

FRANCES *is taken aback as she comprehends*.

FRANCES. But it's the lead review.

MARY. Which is why we need a fall-back position. I'd do it myself, but I'm up to here!

FRANCES *is a little daunted, but...*

FRANCES. Alright. I'll start now.

MARY. And Frances, I know I'm piling things on you…
I promised Audrey Cullum I'd go to this tonight –

She hands her an invitation…

– but I've got to take Leo to the premiere of this new Marvel
movie. He's desperate to meet Lupita Nyong'o.

FRANCES *reads the invite.*

It's a charity thing – an anthology of short stories by
prisoners. I know – yawn. But your friend Laurence Kyte
wrote the foreword. Might get a diary story out of it.

FRANCES *betrays no emotion.*

FRANCES. I can look in. No problem.

MARY. What would I do without you?

FRANCES *laughs.*

FRANCES. You'd manage.

MARY *looks at* FRANCES *for a moment.*

MARY. You look different today, Frances. Pretty.

FRANCES. I'm sorry…?

MARY. Oh, I know we're not supposed to say things like that
any more – but it's true. Don't worry – I'm off to HR now in
any case. I'll report myself.

And MARY *goes off.* FRANCES *has a moment in which to
settle before* ROBIN *arrives – clearly under pressure –*

FRANCES. Robin…?

ROBIN. Dear God, it's like the *Marie Celeste.* Where's your
department?

FRANCES. Oliver's in San Remo for a couple of days, and
Mary's had to leave a bit early… taking her son to see a film.

ROBIN*'s aghast.*

Is there anything I can do to help?

ROBIN. I don't know! Is there? How about... keep the paywall from going any higher and stop the print edition being axed?

FRANCES *faces him down and –*

FRANCES. I did have an idea for a new Books column.

ROBIN. Christ, not now, Laura.

He's about to be on his way again, but...

FRANCES. Laura's in Lifestyle. I'm Frances.

A genuine apology.

ROBIN. Sorry... Frances. *Frances.*

ROBIN *makes to leave but...* FRANCES *asserts herself.*

FRANCES. 'What Page Are You On?'...

ROBIN. Mm?

FRANCES. That's what it's called.

ROBIN. Email me.

FRANCES. I did, months ago.

ROBIN *yields, reluctantly, for a moment.*

ROBIN. I apologise. I get a lot of emails.

FRANCES. Apology accepted. So...?

He breathes, takes her in.

ROBIN. So. 'What Page Are You On?'...

FRANCES *puts her case...*

FRANCES. The idea is to feature people who are famous but not... bookish...

ROBIN. People who people have actually heard of...?

FRANCES. Exactly... an actor... sportsperson... MP...

ROBIN. Katie Price.

FRANCES. The CEO of Coca-Cola, whoever's upped their ad-spend lately...

ROBIN*'s listening now.*

ROBIN. Go on…

FRANCES. We print a stock photo. They tell us the fifth sentence on page fifty of whatever they're reading.

A beat.

ROBIN. That's it? The whole thing.

FRANCES *nods*.

FRANCES. It's fun. A little hook…

ROBIN *considers*.

ROBIN. Get the first three mocked up.

FRANCES. Thank you…

ROBIN. How long have you been here?

FRANCES. Four years. You?

ROBIN*'s surprised by the question.*

ROBIN. Thirty-nine, thanks for asking. My only job before that? Paper boy. I got up at dawn in all weathers and I never resented it once. Because I thought I was doing something important. Delivering the news. Now they don't even wrap chips in it.

He shakes his head.

What do you want for yourself in the future?

FRANCES. I want you to remember my name.

ROBINS *laughs, wheels away, cheered*.

ROBIN. Nice job, Frances.

FRANCES *faces out*.

FRANCES. I head on to Mary's cast-off event. It's not Taittinger and canapés like her Marvel premiere, but there's Sauvignon blanc and Costco crisps.

And a woman – that woman – from Alys's memorial… In the same striped scarf.

A thin blue and white silk scarf appears and dances like
police tape… FRANCES watches it, transfixed, until
AUDREY CULLUM *– a rangey older woman with*
outlandish dress sense – crosses the room. FRANCES
intercepts her –

Audrey Cullum…?

AUDREY *has a strong Estuary accent.*

AUDREY. Yes…?

FRANCES. Frances Thorpe from *The Questioner.* Mary sends
apologies. Something came up at the office.

AUDREY. I bet it did. This isn't her highness's idea of fun.
Least *you* made it.

FRANCES. Glad to be here. It's a good cause.

AUDREY. Exactly!

FRANCES. I think there's a diary piece in it.

AUDREY. Music to my ears.

AUDREY *lowers her voice, cheerfully conspiratorial…*

How are things? At *The Questioner?*

FRANCES. Oh, all fine.

AUDREY *laughs.*

AUDREY. You don't have to put on a brave face for me. We
were on eggshells at *The Recorder* the best part of ten years.
Then this nice Russian chap wrote us a cheque. The paper's
shit. But the mortgage gets paid.

FRANCES. I did hear your new Arts Editor was fresh from
from *Grazia.*

AUDREY. She's about twelve years old. You know what
happened the other day? She stops typing for a moment and
turns to me. She says, 'Audrey – where's the "p" in
"dreamt"?' That's who I report to now.

FRANCES *laughs in commiseration.*

FRANCES. Oh dear…

AUDREY. The 'p' in fucking 'dreamt'!

FRANCES. Audrey, who's that woman in the blue and white scarf?

AUDREY *squints across.*

AUDREY. Julia Price. From Siren Books.

FRANCES. Julia Price. Good to put a face to a name. She did a really good 'In the Footsteps' for us.

AUDREY. The du Maurier piece, I saw it. 'In the Footsteps of *Rebecca*'. Clever little strand that. I bet you pay them peanuts.

FRANCES. Cheap as chips.

AUDREY. Cos it's all about the travel freebie.

FRANCES. Two nights in a romantic boutique hotel on the Cornish coast, I think she had.

AUDREY. And it hardly cost *The Questioner* much more than the train fare. Canny.

FRANCES. Wish I'd thought of it. My colleague Sid's idea.

FRANCES *nods, glances at* JULIA PRICE *again…*

She's striking, isn't she?

AUDREY. Julia's got that thing people can't resist.

FRANCES. What's that?

AUDREY *considers a second, then…*

AUDREY. She's a mystery.

But –

Blimey – there's Obafemi Daramola… I just need to… 'Scuse me, Frances – catch you later.

Then she pats FRANCES*'s arm and moves on… The blue and white scarf dances in the breeze.* FRANCES *faces out.*

FRANCES. So, I'm watching Julia Price and the men hanging off her, when I see her face change.

LAURENCE *enters*.

And the mystery starts to reveal itself.

LAURENCE *freezes at the sight of* JULIA*'s fluttering scarf*.

Come on, Laurence.

LAURENCE *sees* FRANCES, *squints to pull her into focus. He's surprised…*

Look this way. Let me help you off the hook.

He approaches –

LAURENCE. It's Frances, isn't it…?

FRANCES. Laurence.

Awkward pats on the arm.

LAURENCE. I'm so happy to run into you like this… I've wondered about getting in touch…

FRANCES. Oh…?

LAURENCE. You've been so kind to Polly.

FRANCES. Gosh, hardly…

LAURENCE. Oh, please! Above and beyond. I wanted to apologise…

FRANCES. There's really no need.

LAURENCE. Turning up on your doorstep like that… What was she thinking?

FRANCES. I actually enjoy her company. She's rather energising.

LAURENCE *is astonished*.

LAURENCE. Is she? I find her completely exhausting.

FRANCES *laughs*.

FRANCES. Of course you do. You're her father. Everything you say is wrong.

LAURENCE. Any advice I give sends her skittering off in the opposite direction.

FRANCES *laughs*.

But you gave her such a good steer about drama school. The idea of a sabbatical – keeping the door open. Thank God she listened.

FRANCES. I just… helped her come to the decision by herself.

LAURENCE. No doubt the approach her mother would have taken. I'm too clumsy. Oh – here's Teddy…

TEDDY *approaches, eyes* FRANCES, *confused*.

Find somewhere?

TEDDY. Yellow line on Russell Square.

LAURENCE. Great. Y'remember Frances…?

TEDDY. Frances, wow.

TEDDY *nods, politely to her.*

FRANCES. Teddy.

TEDDY. But what brings you here?

FRANCES. Ah… this is awkward. I work on the Arts section of *The Questioner*. The Books page actually.

LAURENCE *is surprised*.

LAURENCE. Really?

FRANCES. Didn't Polly say? It's a little odd, I know. I almost thought I should have mentioned it when we first met, but… that hardly felt… .

LAURENCE. But that's so strange…? To think we've moved in such similar circles – in Suffolk and London. But our paths never crossed.

He glances at his son.

TEDDY. Weird.

FRANCES *shrugs. The ways of fate*.

LAURENCE. But here we are now.

FRANCES. Here we are.

TEDDY *interrupts, discomfited…*

TEDDY. I ought to say hello to Charlotte… I can see her out the back.

LAURENCE. Sure…

TEDDY *nods goodbye, leaves.*

I met a woman from *The Questioner* – quite a while ago now…

FRANCES. Mary Pym…?

LAURENCE. Yes! We were on a panel together. The Sunderland Prize, perhaps?

FRANCES. Mary sent me here tonight to hunt for diary stories. The person who usually does it's away. But gossip's not really my forte. I've spent most of the evening trying to stop people oversharing.

They laugh.

LAURENCE. People like to tell you things.

FRANCES. They seem to.

LAURENCE. You've got that kind of face.

A moment of something before –

I'm afraid to think what Polly's blurted out.

FRANCES. How's Polly doing…?

LAURENCE. Better. On the surface, at least. She's talking about spending time at Biddenbrooke this summer. That'll be hard. She'll feel the loss.

FRANCES. She knows I'm only a phone call away. And how are *you*?

The sincere enquiry gives LAURENCE *pause.*

LAURENCE. Oh – well, I'm… I'm…

But the words don't come.

Actually, this is my first... social anything since... what happened. But I felt I should. A good cause. I truly believe that.

FRANCES. Me too.

LAURENCE. These writers – most of them with terrible backgrounds, endlessly failed by the system. Living in cages... but 'writing their way out'.

FRANCES. That really strikes a chord with you.

LAURENCE. Impossible not to be moved.

FRANCES. Are you writing at the moment?

LAURENCE. No. I mean, not really.

FRANCES. Well, I wish you would.

LAURENCE laughs.

LAURENCE. Do you?

FRANCES shrugs, embarrassed.

FRANCES. I'm a fan.

LAURENCE. Well, I'd better round up Teddy. We should probably slope off. Polly's coming to dinner. I'd invite you, but it's a stab at family bonding.

FRANCES. That's brilliant. What are you cooking?

LAURENCE. Oh – I'm not. No, I've hired a housekeeper. Mrs King. I rather let the domestic stuff go, I'm afraid. I don't think we'll need her forever. But for now... She's very nice.

FRANCES. That sounds a good idea. It's important. To feel looked after.

LAURENCE. Yes. I took it rather for granted. Coming home to the smell of cooking. Such a simple thing, but...

He shakes off the emotion.

Perhaps another time.

FRANCES. Another time?

LAURENCE. Dinner.

FRANCES *smiles sweetly.*

FRANCES. I'd like that.

LAURENCE. Assuming I survive Polly tonight.

FRANCES. You'll be fine. She adores you. Really.

LAURENCE *hesitates a moment.*

LAURENCE. Thank you. For saying that. It means a lot.

He leans in to kiss FRANCES *but she pats his arm and walks away.*

FRANCES. I turn to look back at him just for a moment.

She turns back and LAURENCE *is still watching.*

And there it is, in the air – the shock of possibility.

LAURENCE *and* FRANCES *consider one another. A long moment before* LAURENCE *is released from* FRANCES*'s gaze. He goes off. Now* POLLY *enters, on the phone…*

POLLY. Oh, hi Frances. Polly here. Sorry it's been a while. Just wanted to say – thanks for the advice about college. Bloody good thing I listened. Turns out, the tour's off. It's a disaster. Anyway, I'm at Biddenbrooke. Teddy's here now but he's not sure he's staying. And Dad and Charlotte don't arrive till Monday. There's lots of room. And the thing is…

A moment.

I'm not very good on my own. So come for a bit if you like?

POLLY *goes off. We hear the sound of the sea washing against the shore.*

FRANCES *looks out at us.*

FRANCES. 'Why not?', I think. I'd love to.

Interval.

Chapter Six

FRANCES. It's not long after six. The road shimmers with heat as I turn at the Imberly crossroads.

POLLY *wanders in, on her phone.*

POLLY. Oh that's great, Frances – everyone else I asked is away! – have you got a pen?

FRANCES. I follow – Alys's much-loved route. The one she'll never drive again.

POLLY. You'll see a red phone box, that's where you turn off... Take the track through the meadow, and you'll see my car. A white Mini. One of the new ones, yeah...?

POLLY *leaves.*

FRANCES. I park the Fiat, and sit for a moment, watching the hollyhocks in the breeze.

I'm pretty sure they're hollyhocks.

The front door is locked, so I head round the side...

FRANCES *takes in the garden. Breathtaking.*

I know this view well from my trawl of the *Country Living* archives. A picture of Alys, in a pretty straw hat, poised, camera-shy, with Digitalis Albiflora... Eupatorium Rugosum... Philadelphus Belle Étoile.

A straw hat appears, on a hook with a thin grey shawl and well-used kitchen apron.

The scent of mint as I push past the bushes, step into Alys's kitchen...

FRANCES *sets down her bag, entranced. Lifts the hat from its hook and rests it – oh so carefully – on her head. The moment fills...*

Lights come up on a garden table. On it, a tray with a sparkling glass jug filled with mint-sprigged elderflower cordial. Ice-filled tumblers. We hear voices – combative but humorous. They might be a memory. They might be real. TEDDY *and* POLLY.

POLLY(*offstage*). It was in.

TEDDY(*offstage*). It was not.

POLLY(*offstage*). I thought you could 'hardly see the ball' with the sun in your eyes…? Now, all of a sudden you…

TEDDY and POLLY arrive sweaty, red-faced with tennis racquets. They stop abruptly – take in the sight of the table, readied for them. Bewilderment. Then POLLY grips her racquet like a weapon, unsettled.

Hello…?

TEDDY. Who's there?

The two of them look like frightened children. FRANCES puts the hat back on the hook, turns to them, appearing in the scene now.

FRANCES. Hello.

TEDDY. Jesus… what the fuck?

POLLY. Oh…

POLLY seems a little uncertain… then…

Amazing! You came!

TEDDY. Seriously, Polly?

TEDDY stomps past, barely nodding to FRANCES, and into the house. FRANCES is apologetic –

FRANCES. I'm so sorry – I knocked, but there was no…

POLLY. No – it's me. I've completely lost track.

FRANCES. I guessed you couldn't be far away… The radio was on.

POLLY. We had a quick knockabout next door… They let us use their court, we let them use our beach.

FRANCES. Perhaps I shouldn't have let myself in…?

POLLY. There's a key hanging up in the greenhouse – half North London lets itself in!

FRANCES. But Teddy seemed upset.

POLLY. Oh, don't mind him. God, let's start again –

POLLY flings open her arms –

Woo-hoo! You're here! I won't actually hug you, I'm minging.

FRANCES *laughs.* POLLY *hurries to pour two glasses from the jug.*

And look at this – brilliant. The sprig of mint and everything. Like Mum used to do it.

FRANCES. Really...?

She gives one to FRANCES *– they toast.*

POLLY. Here's to the hols. I thought I'd swim later. Bring a cozzie?

FRANCES. You bet.

POLLY leads her back inside...

POLLY. Your bedroom's on the first floor. A view of the sheep and the croquet lawn.

POLLY suddenly stops.

Shit! Jacob and Marie-Elise were in there last night, and Mrs Talbot the housekeeper doesn't come till Monday. Eugh. We'll have to change the bed...

TEDDY*'s voice rings angrily through the house.*

TEDDY (*offstage*). Polly?!

POLLY (*to* FRANCES). Just grab some clean sheets and pillowcases from the airing cupboard. I won't be a minute.

TEDDY (*offstage*). *Pol...?*

POLLY. Sorry Frances...

FRANCES. I'm fine – really – go...

And POLLY *withdraws to bellow back:*

POLLY. What?!

POLLY *hurries to argue with* TEDDY *face to face*. TEDDY *lowers his voice significantly.*

TEDDY. Are you serious? Her? Of all people.

FRANCES *listens in, intrigued…*

POLLY. Her name's Frances.

TEDDY. It's fucking nuts. Even by your standards.

FRANCES *hovers, listening in…*

POLLY. Hey – she's really been there for me the last few months. And she's good at fitting in. Not like Honor.

TEDDY. Christ, shut up about Honor.

POLLY. I don't remember you asking me if it was okay to invite her?

TEDDY. It's hardly the same. This is… morbid. It's macabre.

But POLLY *pleads with him…*

POLLY. No it's not. Teddy, trust me, it's not. Please, I promise. Come on…

TEDDY *exhales heavily, barely persuaded. He picks up his car keys.* POLLY*'s upset –*

Don't go, Teddy… please…

But he settles her, apparently resigned.

TEDDY. I'm going to buy milk before the shop shuts.

She suddenly hugs him, relieved, but –

Okay, Polly – you're rank.

He holds her at arm's length.

POLLY. I know, I'm sorry…

TEDDY. I mean you're absolutely…

POLLY *laughs, attacks him with her underarms.*

POLLY. I'm going swimming in a minute!

FRANCES *quietly retires. Takes in the house.*

TEDDY. The hydrangeas have all wilted. Get the hosepipe out
and give them a shower. Do yourself at the same time.
Seriously...

He pushes her away from him and hurries out.

POLLY. Aaaaagh!

POLLY *shouts up the stairs, glad to have survived the
encounter with her brother –*

Frances – did you find your room...?

FRANCES. I did. It's really lovely...!

POLLY. Good! I'm doing some watering! Then I'll be up to
help you.

FRANCES. No rush. It's a holiday, after all...

POLLY *goes off. The sound of a car leaving, followed by
running water.*

My room *is* lovely. On the bed, there's a brown apple core
and last week's *Spectator*. But I throw those away.

Polly hasn't told me where the airing cupboard is. So... I have
to have a good look.

FRANCES *directs us...*

Here's her room – rosebud wallpaper pitted with BluTack.
A floordrobe of discarded outfits. And here's Teddy's bolthole,
a condom wrapper, a *Beano* annual. And a packet of
something called citalopram. For anxiety and depression. Hm.

And finally, Laurence and Alys's...

FRANCES *takes in the hallowed space.*

The wardrobe's still full on Alys's side. Bright sundresses.
Tan sandals. High heels with red soles. And here, on the
dresser, a pen-and-ink sketch of the kids, very young... And
a framed wedding photo – the kiss on the steps. Oh, Alys...

The sound of the water stops. Immediately –

POLLY. It was a fuck-up in the end. Pure and simple.

*POLLY – in a bikini – rolls out towels for her and
FRANCES. FRANCES strips down to swimwear. We're at
the beach!*

FRANCES. But that's so disappointing…

POLLY. I know – 'Shakespeare', you think. 'What could
possibly go wrong?'

The women settle down together in the sun.

But it turned out we needed like permits and stuff. Bloody
red tape. Theo just felt his vision was being totally
compromised. It's a bummer.

FRANCES. I'm sorry.

POLLY. I don't mind so much. If I'm honest. It's good, being
here…

FRANCES. Good's an understatement! This is heaven.

POLLY. I feel closer to Mum.

FRANCES takes in POLLY's face.

FRANCES. Oh, I'm sorry – that was thoughtless…

POLLY. No – it's good you feel like that. She always meant to
create… a kind of sanctuary. It really helps me and Teddy to
know we can come, and be with her.

FRANCES absorbs this.

FRANCES. How long have you had the house?

POLLY. Since we got back from the States, pretty much.

FRANCES. You lived in the States?!

POLLY. Oh yeah – Dad wrote some screenplays. So it was
kerching! We'd been poor as church mice before that.
A mildewy rental in Kilburn that still had an outdoor loo!

FRANCES laughs.

But then it was LA, baby! Jamba Juice. Swimming pools.
Lunch at Brad Pitt's.

FRANCES. Sounds great – why didn't you stay?

POLLY. Mum hated it. Said she couldn't understand herself in
a place where there weren't any seasons. We moved back.
They bought the London house, then this place.

A moment, then…

I think about her all the time… Working on her garden.
Or on the terrace, wrapped in her pashmina, planning her
next move.

FRANCES *squeezes* POLLY*'s hand. A companionable
silence, then…*

FRANCES. Polly, are you sure Teddy's okay with me coming?

POLLY. Oh he's just… you know… Anything that reminds him
about what happened is hard. Plus, he's extra pissed off cos
Honor's just gone. I thought he'd leave when she did, but he
hasn't. Which is nice.

FRANCES. Honor's his girfriend?

POLLY. I guess.

FRANCES *laughs*.

We've all known her for years. She used to be okay, but
these days she's a mare. Sunbathes topless on the terrace
every chance she gets – just *willing* my dad to walk in. She's
a total beg. Dad hates it.

FRANCES. Does he?

POLLY. I think she's got some kind of complex. Her dad and
Laurence were pals at uni. Socialist firebrands together – snort.

FRANCES. Why's that so funny?

POLLY. Oh, come on! Dad's idea of manning the barricades
these days is doing the *Guardian* quick crossword and
refusing to let us get Sky TV! But I feel bad for Teddy. His
girlfriends all fall for the Great Man.

Then –

Okay – enough gassing… I'll race you in… But I warn you – it's bloody cold!

And POLLY *scrambles to her feet, rushes off. A splash and screaming laughter.* FRANCES *laughs. She watches a while, soaking up the sun and sea, then collects up their beach stuff as the light fades…*

FRANCES. We have a really lovely day. The sun shines, non-stop. I feel the heat of it deep in my bones. And I feel something else. Something unfamiliar. I realise: it's 'happy'. Later, I cook dinner.

FRANCES *pulls on a fresh dress – a brighter colour than we've seen her in before. Fairy lights come on in a tree. Little candles flicker in lanterns.* POLLY *weaves out, dressed now, with a bottle and two glasses of wine, hands one to* FRANCES.

POLLY. How could you make something so delicious out of leftovers? You're a genius!

FRANCES. It was a joint effort.

POLLY. All Teddy and I did was find Dad's Sancerre.

FRANCES *looks fondly on as* POLLY *collapses happily onto the ground, wine in one hand, spliff in the other.*

Wow… I'm just so relaxed from that swim.

FRANCES. Same.

POLLY. The swim and the wine. And the dinner and the spliff.

FRANCES *settles on the ground not far from* POLLY, *looks up at the night sky.*

FRANCES. Isn't Teddy coming out?

POLLY. He's on the phone. Some crisis at the gallery.

FRANCES. He seems more relaxed…

POLLY. He's fine. Is that Orion's Belt?

FRANCES. Haven't the faintest.

They take it all in… a sense of wonder.

POLLY. Hey, have you got that feeling… that you're falling *up*? Like you might fall into the sky. Could that actually happen…?

FRANCES *starts to laugh.*

I think it could… Don't laugh at me, Frances.

But POLLY*'s starting to laugh along now.*

Why are you laughing…?

FRANCES *and* POLLY *laugh uncontrollably.* TEDDY *arrives.*

TEDDY. What are you cackling about?

POLLY. Witches cackle. We're not witches.

TEDDY *reaches for* POLLY*'s spliff. She hands it over.*

Ohhhhhh… We need music.

She gets up, hurries off. He calls after her –

TEDDY. Nothing tragic…

POLLY. Yeah, yeah…

TEDDY *and* FRANCES *alone.*

TEDDY. It's all hard enough without Leonard Cohen.

He looks away. FRANCES *takes him in.*

FRANCES. Everything alright at work?

TEDDY. Just some bullshit. Hard sometimes to know who's more temperamental – the artists we show or the oligarchs who invest in them.

FRANCES. Both sound pretty tricky.

TEDDY. I've had a lot of experience with difficult temperaments.

Before FRANCES *can enquire further, 'Satellite of Love' by Lou Reed (for example) comes up on a speaker.* TEDDY *calls to* POLLY –

Oh – nice one.

POLLY *dances back out.*

POLLY. Yeah, cos I used a playlist off your phone. You ought to change your passcode.

FRANCES *smiles.*

Dad's is one, two, three, four. That's all he can remember!

They all laugh.

TEDDY. Great with words. Not good with numbers.

TEDDY *passes* FRANCES *the spliff. She hesitates… We see she's unusually loosened up.*

FRANCES. I'm okay, thanks… Just happy with the wine. And the stars. And the moon.

POLLY *dances around her.*

POLLY. Good old Frances. Not much to ask for, is it – the universe!

The others laugh. The music plays on, the lights twinkle. TEDDY walks off a little way, smoking, looks out over the sea. We forget about him. FRANCES watches POLLY twirl. The picture is intoxicating. The world around them darkens further. POLLY collapses happily to the ground, stretches out… FRANCES feels a strange happiness…

FRANCES. Polly…?

POLLY barely registers this… FRANCES ventures, in spite of herself… a heartfelt admission…

This is so lovely.

Nothing from POLLY.

Just being here.

The offering hangs in the air a moment…

With you.

FRANCES looks out into the night, dangerously full of feeling… Darkness closes in until only FRANCES is visible…

It means a lot…

But POLLY *doesn't answer. A powerful sense of* FRANCES*'s aloneness. Until –*

TEDDY. Right, let's get this over with, Frances.

TEDDY *appears from the darkness.* FRANCES *scrambles to catch up with the development...*

FRANCES. Teddy...? I didn't realise you were...

But he looms over her, speaks with dangerous urgency.

TEDDY. I don't know what your game is, but you need to pack your bag. Make up some story about needing to clear out first thing. Shouldn't be too hard. You're good at making things up, after all...

FRANCES. I'm sorry...?

But he cuts her off –

TEDDY. I've been in touch with the police. I know everything.

FRANCES. What do you...?

TEDDY. I asked for a copy of your statement.

FRANCES *begins to understand...*

None of us could face the idea of reading it at the time. But my shrink thought it would be good for me. Closure. That crap. 'Tell them I love them.' She never said that.

FRANCES *admits with some difficulty –*

FRANCES. No.

TEDDY. Although your statement *does* record her saying that she'd had a really awful Christmas.

FRANCES *hangs her head, but her brain races.*

FRANCES. Yes.

TEDDY. You invented my mother's last words.

FRANCES. I'm so sorry – it was a stupid thing to do.

TEDDY. We were total strangers, and you took it upon yourself to lie. To present a completely false...

FRANCES. No – not completely –

TEDDY. A false, false version of events! About something so important…

FRANCES pushes back a little…

FRANCES. Look… When I met you, you were all so… distressed. I just wanted to help… Please… believe me…

But TEDDY *still burns with intensity.*

TEDDY. Oh, I do. You wanted to offer us some kind of comfort. It worked. You made up a story. We loved it. I ought to be grateful.

FRANCES. You don't sound grateful…

TEDDY. Because now it's all about what comes next, isn't it?! You gave us a farewell we could just about live with. Now you need to fuck off so it can stay that way.

FRANCES. Right.

TEDDY*'s becoming unhinged now…*

TEDDY. You need to just disappear. I'd go the shallow-grave route, but we're not allowed to dig here. When we were kids, we couldn't even play football in case we damaged Mum's prized fern collection.

FRANCES. Teddy…

TEDDY *manages a burst of angry finality –*

TEDDY. You see the thing you need to know is, it was right, what Charlotte said about Mum at the memorial. She was just as much the artist as Dad.

FRANCES. I'm sure.

TEDDY. With her white garden and her greengage jam. And her pen-and-ink sketches of her perfect family. She should've won a prize for that – it's the biggest fucking fiction of them all.

He stops now, seems exhausted. And then his shoulders heave and he begins to sob. FRANCES *gathers her courage… Draws a little closer…*

FRANCES. Teddy…? Listen to me… Even though Alys didn't say it… that she loved you… I… believe – absolutely – no matter what you imagine – that it was true.

She goes to touch him… His hand flies up to stop her.

Oh, Teddy…

She tries again and suddenly his arms wrap round her. Overwhelming… Finally, his tears subside. He breaks free.

TEDDY. Fuck…

FRANCES. It's okay.

TEDDY. Fuck…

FRANCES. I'm sorry. I'll pack. Forgive me.

He's exhausted. Lost.

TEDDY. God, what's the difference?

He shakes his head.

You might as well stay… I need to get Polly to bed.

FRANCES *acknowledges this.* TEDDY *lifts* POLLY, *carries her off…* FRANCES *watches them go, reeling. Looks out.*

FRANCES. The next day, I resolve to drink much less with dinner.

She breathes, reorientates.

I'm first up. I leaf through old cookbooks while the kettle boils. Note Alys's careful handwritten additions – 'needs an extra fifteen minutes…', 'too many capers… not enough lemon…'

An electronic buzzing sound – texts coming in on a mobile phone.

Teddy's phone, left out from last night…

FRANCES *quickly inspects the phone. A moment of calculation, then* FRANCES *quickly pulls an apron off a hook, ties it on –*

I decide to bake a pie.

FRANCES *pushes up her sleeves, zhuzhes her hair with more oomph than baking strictly requires. A shaft of sunlight from an unexpected direction – she turns and is bathed in it – picture perfect.*

LAURENCE *stands looking at her from the open doorway. It's a long charged moment, then –*

Chapter Seven

FRANCES *laughs along with* POLLY, TEDDY, FRANCES *and* CHARLOTTE *as* LAURENCE *holds court at a very happy al fresco dinner. The sun just going down. The sound of the sea in the distance.*

LAURENCE. Poor Frances – caught completely on the hop – flour all over her face…

The others laugh. FRANCES *takes off the apron, affects comedy embarrassment.*

FRANCES. I can't imagine what I looked like!

LAURENCE. The most marvellous smell curling right through the house.

CHAROLOTTE. You two still in bed!

POLLY. You weren't supposed to be here till tomorrow…

LAURENCE. We had to get out. London's baking. Impossible to work. And I messaged you both first thing…

POLLY. Who does 'first thing' on holiday?!

TEDDY. When you say 'work'…? Are we talking…?

CHARLOTTE *raises her hands, urging caution…*

CHARLOTTE. Softly, softly…

TEDDY. Sorry – I didn't mean to…

But LAURENCE *reassures his son –*

LAURENCE. It's fine. Early days… Just noodling about a bit.

TEDDY. I think that's great.

POLLY. Me too.

POLLY *hugs* LAURENCE. *She explains to* FRANCES.

Dad couldn't see the point in writing after Mum died. That's right, isn't it?

LAURENCE. I couldn't think who I was writing for. Alys was always my first reader.

LAURENCE*'s mood seems to dip a little.* CHARLOTTE *pats his hand…*

CHARLOTTE. Alright – I don't like talk about work in progress. It lets in too much light.

POLLY. Mum used to say that planting and writing had a lot in common. All the important work happens in the dark.

FRANCES. That's beautiful.

TEDDY *quickly stands. Collects dishes.*

TEDDY. I'll take these. Pol, get your side.

A concession from TEDDY *as he leaves –*

Nice pie, Frances.

FRANCES. Thank you, Teddy.

He heads in, followed by POLLY. CHARLOTTE *and* FRANCES *get up to help too, but are waved back down by* LAURENCE, *who stacks more dishes.*

LAURENCE. No, no, no. You've done enough. The pie was an absolute knock-out.

CHARLOTTE. Yes indeed.

FRANCES. There'd been so many windfalls overnight. I couldn't stand the thought of the fruit going to waste.

LAURENCE. Now, I'm sorry to be dull, but do you mind very much if I turn in?

CHARLOTTE. Of course not. I can lock up. And I'm glad to have Frances to myself.

She turns to FRANCES.

You'll sit out a little longer, won't you...?

Before FRANCES *can answer.*

LAURENCE. Oh dear, now I'm worried!

CHARLOTTE *turns back to* LAURENCE.

CHARLOTTE. Goodnight, my lovely love...

FRANCES *observes, mildly repelled, as* LAURENCE *and* CHARLOTTE *kiss chastely on the lips.* LAURENCE *turns to* FRANCES.

LAURENCE. I'll be working from first thing, so there may not be chance to say goodbye. But I'll see you in London, perhaps?

FRANCES. I hope so.

FRANCES *smiles at him, and he smiles back, a little awkward.* CHARLOTTE *sees everything.*

LAURENCE. Have fun with your parents.

He embraces her. Then –

You've caught the sun. It suits you.

He picks up the dishes, goes... TEDDY *meets him, takes the dishes and herds him indoors. Then the women are left alone.* CHARLOTTE *waits only a moment before...*

CHARLOTTE. It's strange. You're almost part of the family.

FRANCES. I don't know about that.

CHARLOTTE. Even Teddy's taken to you! An unusual way to get to know the Kytes.

FRANCES *bristles slightly.*

FRANCES. A terrible way. It's appalling, what they've been through.

CHARLOTTE. That goes without saying. What we've all been through. You very much included.

FRANCES. It's hardly the same.

CHARLOTTE. Not the same, but… Well, an experience like this changes you. Surely, it has to.

CHARLOTTE *seems at pains to be warmer now.* FRANCES *considers.*

FRANCES. Perhaps that's right. It was a terrible shock at the time, but…

CHARLOTTE*'s intrigued now, waits…*

I will say it's made me less… timid, perhaps? More aware. Of the opportunity of life. Is that an awful thing to admit?

CHARLOTTE. Not at all.

FRANCES. It seems wrong when Polly and Teddy are still so…

CHARLOTTE *interrupts –*

CHARLOTTE. They'll survive this. They had such blessed lives before.

FRANCES. Did they? It certainly looks like that. From the outside.

CHARLOTTE. Oh, they're… flakey, of course. That's their generation. But a very firm foundation to build on. From the moment they were born.

FRANCES. Have you known the Kytes that long?

CHARLOTTE. Heavens yes.

CHARLOTTE *gets to her feet.*

You'll have to excuse me. My hips are seized up from the drive… Will you walk a little?

FRANCES *gets up and follows as* CHARLOTTE *takes a few steps deeper into the garden.*

When Laurence was still up at Oxford, he sent a short story to the Charlotte Black Agency. It came with a very seductive covering letter, telling how his father died young from TB, his mother raised him on her own, working shifts in the local brewery. Books were his way out... He seemed so determined to... become himself.

FRANCES *pays attention.*

I couldn't resist helping him. Gave him a job in the holidays, answering phones. He was useless on the switchboard. But he did win the Williams Prize the following year.

FRANCES. That's a wonderful story.

CHARLOTTE. Long before the children. Before Alys, come to that. I've taken good care of him ever since. And will do to my dying breath! Even though he doesn't always make it easy.

They look out, over the sea.

FRANCES. It's quite a view, isn't it... In the moonlight...

CHARLOTTE. You know, I've seen your byline a lot just lately. Started to look out for it, actually. Your review of the Sturges Hardcastle was terrific.

FRANCES. That's kind.

CHARLOTTE. You've spread your wings and found a favourable wind. Clever girl.

FRANCES. Lucky really.

CHARLOTTE. I don't believe in luck. Preparation plus opportunity – that's luck.

CHARLOTTE *takes* FRANCES *in, considers a moment.*

The paperback of *Affliction* is out next month.

FRANCES. I suppose it's about time...

CHARLOTTE. Ideally, I'd sell the film rights before then, but I'm struggling to do the deal the book deserves. I don't suppose you'd consider re-reviewing it?

FRANCES *struggles with the idea...*

FRANCES. Goodness... that would be hard to justify...

CHARLOTTE. Of course it would. I knew. Forget I asked...

FRANCES. If Laurence would consider an interview, that would be different.

CHARLOTTE. He won't – he's adamant. It's all too connected to Alys...

FRANCES. And any interviewer worth their salt would want him to talk about what happened.

CHARLOTTE. Well I think he *ought* to talk about it. It's as if he's paralysed, somehow. Although *you* might get through to him. Get things moving again...

FRANCES *hears this.*

FRANCES. I'll give it some thought.

CHARLOTTE *presses her hands together in a prayer of gratitude.*

CHARLOTTE. Thank you, Frances.

CHARLOTTE *seizes on something –*

And perhaps I can help you in return. Do you know Audrey Cullum?

FRANCES. At *The Recorder*?

CHARLOTTE. She may be hiring. Her deputy's ill.

FRANCES. Oh, I'm sorry...

CHARLOTTE. They're looking for 'cover' – but the poor girl won't be back. Not with Stage 4 pancreatic. Could you see yourself moving...?

FRANCES *is wrongfooted*.

FRANCES. I don't know…

CHARLOTTE. I can quietly mention your name to Audrey. It can't do any harm… You can take it from there.

Now – bedtime. You've given me so much to think about… And I'm still longing to know your secret.

CHARLOTTE *starts back toward the house, her hip still stiff.*

FRANCES. My secret?

CHARLOTTE. With pastry. You must have cool hands.

FRANCES *watches* CHARLOTTE *head on, out of sight, then faces out.*

FRANCES. There's no secret to the pastry. A light touch, no hurry, lots of air.

Wait for the moment when the texture changes.

The night is so hot, I can't sleep at all. So I pack, for the morning. A few things to remember the time by. Bits and pieces the Kytes won't miss…

Chapter Eight

The Thorpe family garden. MRS THORPE *appears, holding out* ALYS*'s pashmina.*

MRS THORPE. Is this yours, Frances? Hanging on the stairs…?

FRANCES takes it, puts it on.

It is a pretty colour. And so soft…

FRANCES. It's a pashmina. Cashmere.

MRS THORPE. Does it wash?

MR THORPE arrives…

MR THORPE. Biddenbrooke?

FRANCES. Just for the weekend.

FRANCES looks around.

The garden looks different.

MRS THORPE. No Busy Lizzies this year.

MRS THORPE goes out again. As she leaves –

It was a gamble, but sometimes you've just got to hold your nerve.

MR THORPE. The Howards moved to Biddenbrooke. Their son Mark's with the Office of Fair Trading.

Miraculously, FRANCES*'s phone buzzes. She checks it. She smiles.*

Hester heard him on *You and Yours* last week, talking about extended warranties.

MRS THORPE returns with a tray of cheese and biscuits.

MRS THORPE. I don't think we'll have many more days like this. The season's on the turn. Brie or Boursin, dear?

FRANCES. I am sorry – I'm afraid I have to go.

MRS THORPE *is surprised. But* FRANCES *is radiant, full of new energy.*

I've got such a lot to get on with.

FRANCES *turns, absolutely ready for this, to* MARY *who's hurrying to meet her.*

MARY. Frances, can this wait? I mean I'm really…

FRANCES. No.

OLIVER *sorts the day's review copies.* FRANCES *leads* MARY *out of his earshot.*

OLIVER. *Mindfulness for Management.* Christ! *Angling for Pleasure and Profit.*

FRANCES. Audrey Cullum.

MARY. I love Audrey to bits, but…

FRANCES. She's offered me a job. To start straight away.

MARY. The fucking cow.

OLIVER. *The End of Ageing: Lose Ten Years in Ten Days.*

MARY *glances at* OLIVER, *furtive. Nods for* FRANCES *to follow her out of earshot.*

MARY. Deputy Books Editor. My deputy.

FRANCES. But that's Oliver's job.

MARY. Don't be dim, Frances. He got into a fist fight with Emma Radcliffe at the Canongate party. What's worse, he lost! I need someone who can write, edit, commission and sub. Plus all the tweeting and podding that Robin's so keen on. Someone who understands algorithms. But can also behave in public. Who doesn't think *they*'re the story.

FRANCES *considers, clear-eyed.*

FRANCES. What about the money?

MARY. I can match Audrey's offer. Maybe slightly improve on it.

FRANCES *looks out, takes her time.* MARY *leaves her to it.*
FRANCES *rearranges her hair, then returns to the office.*
OLIVER *drags the Ikea bag of rejected review copies across
the room.*

OLIVER. It was actually *brilliant* fun.

FRANCES. Sounds it.

OLIVER. But Christ, I'm paying for it now. I had a quiet pint of
Tristram Shandy. But then I couldn't resist the Margarita
Atwoods… You've not got a cheeky ibuprofen in your bag?

FRANCES. Sorry…

OLIVER*'s phone rings. He pauses* FRANCES *to answer
the call.*

OLIVER. Hello…?

Now he's entirely focused on the call…

Right. Sure.

He hangs up.

Robin's office. I suggested a new column last week.
Probably just wants to talk it over.

FRANCES. Yeah.

He walks to ROBIN*'s fish tank, where* ROBIN *is waiting,
with* MARY *and someone from HR.* FRANCES *watches him
go. As does the rest of the office. Then she looks out.*

Later, my promotion is announced.

SID *from TV and Travel races around his desk, fists aloft in
triumph.*

SID. Get in!

He quickly stops when –

OLIVER *returns – briefly. Clears his desk into a bag.*

OLIVER. Fuck's sake, people – it's a sinking ship. Losing a few
rats isn't going to change that.

Then he's gone. It's as if he never existed.

SID. Pub to celebrate?

FRANCES. Love to but I'm waiting to see Robin. He's just firing Architecture…

SID. Friday, maybe?

FRANCES. Sure.

They're about to part.

SID. Hey, Frances – your hair looks nice. Different. Foxy.

SID *instantly regrets this. But* FRANCES *is kind. Just enough of a shy smile to shade into flirting. He leaves, quickly, hands shoved into his pockets.* ROBIN *arrives.*

ROBIN. 'At Home with Laurence Kyte'? I mean, even last year, I'd have said yes, fantastic… but with sales in freefall, is he sexy enough?

FRANCES *talks fast.*

FRANCES. Well that's exactly the question. We do a career retrospective… The incredible highs – the Booker Prize, Day-Lewis's Oscar. And then the lows…

ROBIN. Sciatica and dwindling sales?

FRANCES. Worse – a sense of total irrelevance. Not just for him – it's all those guys who dominated the landscape… I mean, look at Kyte's books –

ROBIN. I loved *Time's Revenge*…

FRANCES. Yes, but they're all the same after that… White, middle-aged, middle-class men struggle with the decline in their physical powers… a decline which mirrors the state of the culture around them. Who cares about them now?

ROBIN. Yeah, that's good… but not enough.

FRANCES. There's human interest too…

ROBIN. The dead wife?

FRANCES. Wife, companion, muse. Will he write again without her? A beauty, as it happens.

ROBIN*'s intrigued –*

ROBIN. Was she?

FRANCES. English rose, came from money.

ROBIN. Okay… interesting… are there photos? Of her?

FRANCES. Bikini shots in St Tropez.

ROBIN *smiles, considers, then –*

ROBIN. Frances. Can you make him cry?

FRANCES *takes* ROBIN *in. The deal is done.* FRANCES *hurries to –*

FRANCES. There's autumn in the air as I arrive at Laurence's. I've brought our best photographer, a list of open questions and a very good single malt.

LAURENCE*'s London home.* LAURENCE *tops up his glass from a bottle of whisky. We don't see the photographer. We might hear the shutter, see some of the shots.*

LAURENCE. I never quite know how novels begin.

LAURENCE *looks to* FRANCES… *will she have a top-up? He pours for her.*

Sometimes you start with a sentence. Sometimes it's something you hear someone say. Or you get stuck on an image that holds your interest for some reason, you can't work out why. And then you realise you have to write to find out what it means.

FRANCES. And, do you think about the reader…? I mean do you have someone in mind…?

LAURENCE. Well, my first reader was my mother. She thought everything I did was magic. And I wanted to make her proud.

FRANCES *laughs.*

And then, I suppose, I wrote for Alys… I knew she was there.

He stumbles… tops up his drink again.

You know, I led an absolutely charmed life… I didn't realise. And without her… if I'm honest, I don't know whether I can do it…

He glances down at his hands. Can't continue.

FRANCES. But surely this isn't what she would have wanted?

He shrugs. FRANCES *raises her own emotional temperature…*

Your work was, in a sense, a shared project. So surely, you owe it to her – and to your mother – the people who really believed in you – to continue. To work again… to thrive…

FRANCES *waits… Finally – a terrible sob. She sits with him for a moment, then squeezes his shoulder and walks away, discreetly leaving him to his distress.*

This will be the Arts front, no question. I imagine my sister Hester happening on it while she's looking for offers on Winter Sun. That'll spoil her Sunday.

FRANCES *pulls on her coat.* LAURENCE *begins to come to, recover himself. He works his way back to the present, loosened up with Scotch.*

LAURENCE. I'm so sorry… that was… I mean… Wow, that was… I feel lighter, you know.

FRANCES. Really…? Because I was worried… that I'd pushed you too far.

He's working towards euphoric.

LAURENCE. No – I just hadn't realised the extent to which… well the burden… Of what happened.

FRANCES. I feel responsible…

LAURENCE. No – something's lifted. God…

He seems genuinely amazed by the relief he feels.

It's… wow… Truly. I've been so shut down… Not feeling anything. Such a terrible numbness, but… suddenly…

FRANCES. Pain.

LAURENCE. No – *life*! Overwhelming.

A moment of great intensity between them. FRANCES
breaks it.

FRANCES. Well, I've really done enough damage. I'm going to
leave you to recover in peace.

LAURENCE *doesn't want this.*

LAURENCE. No – don't go. Or at least, let me walk you home.

FRANCES *laughs…*

FRANCES. There's really no need.

LAURENCE. I want to.

He touches her sleeve… Her voice is quieter…

FRANCES. It's too far and it's raining…

LAURENCE. Don't go out in the rain…

FRANCES. I've got an umbrella…

LAURENCE. Frances… stay with me.

LAURENCE *tentatively reaches to touch her cheek… Then
he bends down to kiss her… and after a moment of apparent
indecision…* FRANCES *kisses him back…*

Stay with me. Say yes. Say yes.

He walks a couple of steps, holds out his hand to her…
FRANCES *smiles. She's so saying yes.*

*He keeps walking away, smiling and holding out that hand…
Until, once he's out of sight,* FRANCES *faces out.*

FRANCES. I say yes. It rains all night.

(*With clear sexual innuendo.*) I mean, it really pours.

We hear thunder and lightning.

Chapter Nine

The storm finally gives way to light rain at dawn. The Highgate house is quiet. Somewhere nearby, a man is snoring.

FRANCES. Bare feet on an oatmeal stair carpet. I've learned these last weeks what a heavy sleeper Laurence is.

Here's his phone. One, two, three, four. Direct lines for the great and the good. But not for Julia Price. I deleted her a while back.

LAURENCE *enters, still getting dressed.*

You can talk to me about her, you know?

LAURENCE. About?

FRANCES. Alys, of course.

LAURENCE. Why would you say that?

FRANCES. You were quiet this morning… thinking about something. I just felt as though it might be her.

LAURENCE. Oh – no… I was thinking about the book… I'm really getting somewhere now.

He kisses her.

You've brought me back to life. Now, darling, I'm sorry to shoo you away… But Mrs King will be here very shortly. I don't want to shock her.

FRANCES. Heaven forbid… Your guilty secret out…

LAURENCE. Exactly!

They kiss again.

Listen, I've been thinking. Maybe we could meet at your place for a while.

FRANCES. Sure…

LAURENCE. My neighbours are so bloody nosy. I really don't want anyone getting wind of this.

FRANCES. Not a problem.

LAURENCE. Fantastic.

LAURENCE *leaves*. FRANCES *watches him go*.

MARY. What are you up to?

FRANCES *turns to see* MARY – *we're at* The Questioner *now*.

FRANCES. I don't know what you mean…

MARY. You've got a look about you.

MARY*'s mood quickly collapses as she glances around – a moment of panic*.

Oh god, where am I supposed to work today?! This fucking hot-desking is hell. It's like *The Hunger Games* but with Post-It notes. And carrying everything in every day is honestly starting to break my back.

FRANCES. I bagsed you a place first thing. Don't worry.

MARY. Frances, you're an angel.

FRANCES. Over in the far corner.

MARY *worries*.

MARY. Can Robin see me over there?

FRANCES. Oh… probably not. You can swap with me, but I'm right outside the gents' loo?

MARY. Christ, no. *Thank* you. Well he knows I'm in…

MARY *picks up her heavy bags*.

Oh – I hear Charlotte Black sold the film rights for *Affliction*?

FRANCES. Yes, that popped up in my newsfeed too…

MARY. *And* Laurence invited onto *Desert Island Discs*. She should put you on commission. And he should be very grateful!

FRANCES *shrugs, modest to a fault, and* MARY *staggers off in search of her desk.*

FRANCES *looks out –*

FRANCES. Grateful? Hm.

We move back to FRANCES*'s flat.*

The day Laurence comes to my flat for the first time, I box up a few things. Alys's pashmina. A tortoiseshell hairpin. The shoes with the red soles. I drop them, sadly, at the Oxfam shop. Then I crease the spines of the Laurence Kyte novels I haven't got around to yet.

She shrugs, then suddenly –

Laurence Kyte!

LAURENCE *appears, looks guilty…*

You were checking my bookshelves.

LAURENCE. I was. It's true. I needn't have worried.

FRANCES. I told you, I'm your greatest fan.

LAURENCE. You know what? I like it here.

FRANCES. The flat?

LAURENCE. I'm almost jealous.

FRANCES. Jealous? Of the crack-den neighbours or the asbestos in the old Artex ceilings?

He looks up at the ceiling…

LAURENCE. Not really? Asbestos? I think that's illegal…

FRANCES. Yes, the landlord and I are aware of that. It's reflected in the rent. How else could I afford to live here?

LAURENCE. Christ, housing in London's a bloody disgrace. Rough sleepers all over Piccadilly. You've got to step over them to get into Hatchards. Thank goodness we bought our place when we did. Couldn't afford it now. Never mind the Fulham flat.

FRANCES. You own Polly's place?

LAURENCE. Yeah. I mean it's tiny. And Fulham wasn't
Fulham when we bought it. But still.

He looks up at the ceiling.

I am worried about that asbestos.

FRANCES. Apparently it's harmless unless you disturb it.

LAURENCE. I'm the same.

FRANCES *laughs, climbs on top of him.*

No, but I like this area. Edgy. You can be anonymous in
a place like this.

They canoodle.

I miss that. I really do… Yeah, we're definitely better
meeting here.

FRANCES *takes him in. A heavy pause. Something in the
air, it seems, but –*

Refill?

FRANCES. Sure.

FRANCES *slides off him.* LAURENCE *takes her glass, goes
to top it up.*

We only meet at my place now. Weekends fall into a routine.
On Friday, on the way home from work, I pick up croissants
for breakfast. And the coffee Laurence drinks at home. It's
all quite acceptable. Till it's not.

LAURENCE *enters with two glasses of wine.*

LAURENCE. I am sorry. These Christmas parties are a menace.
I mean it's still November! I wouldn't go to this Burberry one
– I mean Burberry, I don't even know why I'm on the list. But
I've promised to take Charlotte. And the next couple of
weekends are chock-a-block. Maybe even the one after that…

He hands her the glass, strokes her hair…

FRANCES. It's crazy.

LAURENCE. Are you going to the Faber drinks?

FRANCES. No.

LAURENCE. Random House?

FRANCES....Mary usually does those.

LAURENCE. I was thinking we might overlap there at least.

FRANCES. Actually. I was just wondering... My parents have been asking what I'm doing for Christmas. And I realised I didn't know.

A moment before he understands – he's appalled.

LAURENCE. Surely you didn't think we'd spend it together?

FRANCES *works swiftly to manage the rebuff.*

FRANCES. Of course not! Well not as such. I just...

LAURENCE. It's our first without Alys. The children's first Christmas without their mother.

FRANCES. Completely. It's just that I'm nearby, in Frynborough. I thought we might sneak in a Boxing Day walk.

LAURENCE *understands –*

LAURENCE. Oh, I'm sorry... You thought we were going to Biddenbrooke...? No! No, we couldn't face that. Darling, we'll be in London.

FRANCES. Ah...

LAURENCE. The kids need their friends – so do I, come to that. No, Biddenbrooke's out of the question.

FRANCES. Of course.

He sees the hurt on FRANCES's face.

LAURENCE. Don't be a goose. You and I will have our own celebration.

FRANCES. Will we...?

LAURENCE. You bet. God, I don't know how I'd have got through this year without you.

FRANCES. Oh, Laurence… is that true?

LAURENCE. You matter very much. I'll miss you through these next few weeks…

> FRANCES *absorbs this moment of emotion. They sit in it for a while. It feels significant.*

Here's to you – and us.

> *They raise their glasses – clink. A humming sound gradually comes up and then turns into –*

> *Dance music at a Christmas party.* CHARLOTTE *appears on the edge of it and beckons to* LAURENCE, *who hurries to join her – she leads him off, heading somewhere much grander… just as* OLIVER *lurches on with a glass of wine. On his head, he wears felt antlers with mistletoe strung through.*

OLIVER. Frances…? Hey – I thought it was you! Don't tell me – Mary sent you fishing for diary stories?

FRANCES. Something like that. How are you?

OLIVER. Brilliant. Yeah.

FRANCES. What are you up to?

OLIVER. Oh, y'know. Fun stuff. Bits of radio, telly. The odd restaurant review. Probably going to do a book.

FRANCES. Wow. What kind of book?

OLIVER. Biography.

FRANCES. Amazing. Of?

OLIVER. My dad. Actually.

FRANCES. Right…

> FRANCES *stifles a smile.*

OLIVER. Ah, there it is, Frances – that condescending smile. Well, we can't all be as brilliant as you.

FRANCES *raises her glass – a parting gesture.*

FRANCES. Goodnight, Oliver.

OLIVER. No – listen – I'm happy to see you doing so well. You've worked really hard to get where you are. Other people are just jealous.

FRANCES. Other people?

OLIVER. Of your thing with the Kytes. When they say 'ambulance chaser', I tell them where to get off.

FRANCES *stiffens.*

FRANCES. That's decent of you.

OLIVER. It is amazing, though? That you only got in there because you'd witnessed that accident? I mean, the dumb fucking luck!

FRANCES. I didn't witness the accident. I was first on the scene. And I sat with Alys Kyte until she died. I wouldn't call it lucky.

OLIVER. Sure, no...

FRANCES. And forgive me if I've tried to help the Kytes. They're completely broken by this. She was everything to them.

He smirks.

OLIVER. Er, not quite.

FRANCES. I'm sorry?

OLIVER. Oh, come on, Frances. You must have heard the rumours – he always had some young thing on the side.

FRANCES *lets this sink in...*

Charlotte Black used to cover for him, but everybody knew... So watch yourself...

A new terrible marvellous thought strikes OLIVER.

Oh God, don't tell me it's too late…!

He's almost hysterical with happiness.

FRANCES. Merry Christmas, Oliver.

She stares him down, seething. He races off, delighted with his evening's work.

FRANCES *faces out, still full of murderous energy.*

Like any family, mine has its Christmas traditions. The most hallowed of which is that it must be a scarring ordeal. Hester must be praised to the skies for bringing prosecco-flavoured crisps. Her husband, once pissed, must stand too close and ask me whether there's anyone special.

And though I had thought this year would be different, I can see now that it won't.

So on Christmas morning, at the Imberly crossroads, I do not take the Frynbrorough road.

There's a key hanging up in the greenhouse in Biddenbrooke. Half North London knows that. And now so do I.

She's inside the Biddenbrooke house now.

I spend Christmas Day eating Alys's chutney, imagining the other girls over the years. The girls who wrote poetry, or did research. The girls in PR, with bright eyes and dark flats, who asked nothing of him. While Alys was here, with her cake tins and jelly moulds.

Those girls have no place in his future.

Chapter Ten

FRANCES*'s flat.* LAURENCE *is here –*

LAURENCE. Wretched. In a word.

FRANCES goes to embrace him.

FRANCES. I'm sorry. I did think of you all.

LAURENCE. That was good of you. I mean, people were marvellous. Berenice's on the twenty-fifth, Sturges's on Boxing Day. They really tried to give us a Christmas. But… God, the anniversary itself…

FRANCES. The children must have been heartbroken.

LAURENCE. Polly cried and cried. Of course. Teddy seemed awfully low too, putting on a brave face. I feel dreadful saying it, but it was a relief when we all went our separate ways.

FRANCES. Your own grief is hard enough to bear. Never mind theirs.

LAURENCE. Thank goodness for Polly's new boyfriend. And Teddy's got Honor. Lovely girl.

FRANCES. Is she…?

LAURENCE. Anyway – it's over. That's the main thing. Thank God. And I've had a clear-out.

FRANCES. Of?

LAURENCE. Alys's things.

FRANCES is surprised.

FRANCES. But why…?

LAURENCE. It had to be done. It was time. And actually…

FRANCES. What?

LAURENCE. Oh, just something rather odd happened.

He hesitates, a little unnerved.

Mrs Talbot called on the twenty-seventh. She'd gone round to Biddenbroke, and she said... Well it's nonsense, of course. But... she felt as though someone had been in the house...

FRANCES*'s eyes open wide.*

FRANCES. A burglar...?

LAURENCE. No. Not that. Nothing was missing. But... Some of Alys's things had been moved around. Odd, intimate things. It gave the poor woman the willies. I just thought – that's it. It's all got to go. Her husband helped her. And I asked Mrs King to do the London house. Couldn't face it. A coward, I know.

FRANCES. I feel sad about this...

LAURENCE *cringes away from* FRANCES*'s emotion.*

LAURENCE. No, no – please don't... Oh, darling – I almost forgot...

He hands her a giftbag.

Merry Christmas!

She pulls out a scarf – it's a winter scarf, but bears the same blue and white stripes as the one we saw on JULIA PRICE. *Ghastly.* FRANCES *covers her horror.*

I thought it was cheering. And *young.*

FRANCES. It's lovely.

LAURENCE. Cashmere.

She kisses him.

Are you peckish? I might grab the takeaway menus...?

LAURENCE *gets up.* FRANCES *faces out.*

FRANCES. It is cashmere. Five per cent. It goes nicely with the lovely gift I received from Mary Pym. Some bath salts from The White Company, slightly dusty. I force myself to wear it.

And as the New Year rolls on, and Laurence's novel grows, little things begin to annoy me: when he listens to the radio, the volume is too high. The way his hair thins at the temple. His skin, sometimes, is just too soft.

LAURENCE *returns to* FRANCES.

LAURENCE. The Thai place was quite good last time, wasn't it? Or sushi?

FRANCES *doesn't respond. The atmosphere has cooled.*

What's wrong?

FRANCES. Nothing.

LAURENCE. Frances?

FRANCES. It's nothing.

LAURENCE. I've done something, haven't I? Tell me…

FRANCES*'s eyes fill with tears.*

FRANCES. No… No, it's us. Hiding away. Cooped up in this flat all the time.

LAURENCE. Oh darling… No!

FRANCES. I don't want to be your guilty secret. It's such an awful feeling.

LAURENCE. But this is terrible.

FRANCES. I'm sorry, it makes me so miserable.

LAURENCE. I can't bear it! When you've made me so happy…

FRANCES. Have I, though…?

LAURENCE. Just when I'd almost lost faith in happiness! Frances, I don't want the children to know. You understand why. It feels too soon.

FRANCES. Yes, of course. I do see that…

LAURENCE. But I can't have you miserable. What would make you feel better?

FRANCES. Oh… ignore me. I'm just being silly.

LAURENCE. I seem to have ignored you for too long already!

LAURENCE *has a big idea.*

Let's go out to supper.

FRANCES. Somewhere 'low-key'? 'Out of the way...'? It's alright – I'll cook something for us. I can't face any more takeaway...

LAURENCE. No! Somewhere in town. Somewhere nice.

FRANCES *seems hardly to believe her luck... dries her tears.*

FRANCES. Are you sure?

LAURENCE. Absolutely! You decide. Where would you *really* like to go?

Chapter Eleven

Morning. MARY *sweeps into* The Questioner *office dragging a small case on wheels and waving a copy of* Metro.

MARY. Well, well, well... who's this stepping out of The Ivy.

FRANCES. Don't! I was mortified. Can you actually recognise me? I thought I was hidden?

MARY. Not quite. In any case, the lovely scarf gave you away.

FRANCES *clutches at the hideous item.*

FRANCES. It was perfectly quiet when we went in. Then Idris Elba and Sienna Miller arrived.

MARY. Together?

FRANCES. I don't think so – but these shots can make anything look like anything. At least no one reads *Metro*.

Something's happening in ROBIN*'s glass box. He's waving at them as he phones someone.* MARY*'s phone rings... she answers. We see* ROBIN *talking, very entertained.* MARY *repeats for* FRANCES –

MARY. Oh dear... it's in the Mail Online...

FRANCES *affects horror.*

FRANCES. Not the Sidebar of Shame...?

ROBIN *hangs up on* MARY, *gives a 'thumbs-up' to* FRANCES. MARY *relays* –

MARY. 'Kiss me Kyte: Second Shot at Happiness for Tragic Brainbox'. Robin's ecstatic.

FRANCES *covers her face...* MARY*'s mindful of* ROBIN, *needs to start work...*

No, no, no – pay no attention – it's just friends out to dinner. Isn't that right?

FRANCES. That exactly.

FRANCES *observes* MARY*'s case on wheels.*

Mary, are you going somewhere?

MARY. Ha! I wish! My back's out, with all this carrying.

FRANCES. Shall I book you in with the osteopath? The chap in Welbeck Street?

MARY. Oh, that would be saintly.

FRANCES. I'll see if he can't get you in later today.

FRANCES*'s phone receives a text message.*

It's Laurence. He's in reception. And... sorry, Mary, you've got a bit of... I think it's just Gaviscon...

FRANCES *indicates* MARY*'s lip.* MARY *quickly covers her mouth, hurries off.*

FRANCES *faces out.*

Light cool hands, no hurry, lots of air. Wait for the moment when the texture changes.

LAURENCE *rushes in, waving a copy of* Metro.

LAURENCE. It's alright, don't panic. I've thought it through. I need to tell the children. Christ, they're not children! I should stop saying that. They're young adults. And surely they want me to be happy? And you make me happy. So.

FRANCES *is taken aback.*

I thought you'd be more excited.

FRANCES. I am excited.

LAURENCE. You don't seem it…

FRANCES. I am, but…

LAURENCE. But what…?

FRANCES. Surely, if they see this, and recognise me… We're just two friends having dinner. I don't think you should say anything more to them.

LAURENCE. Really?

FRANCES. Well, look at it from their point of view. Teddy and Polly won't want to know that you have some casual 'girlfriend'. It would seem like… I don't know… a betrayal of their mother.

LAURENCE. Go on…

LAURENCE *listens…*

FRANCES. To take this step… we'd have to be sure about our relationship. Really sure.

He's taken aback.

LAURENCE. But I am.

FRANCES. You don't have to say that…

LAURENCE. I'm not… I've been sure for ages…!

FRANCES *appears unconvinced. But he means it –*

Since that day when I arrived at Biddenbroke... you were there in the kitchen and... do you remember? I startled you. You were baking. And something happened, a sort of electricity...

FRANCES *tilts her head, a little vague...*

You haven't got a clue what I'm talking about!

FRANCES. No, I have...

LAURENCE. Darling – you're such a useless liar! I'm more than sure. I'm glad this has happened. I want this.

FRANCES. Long term?

LAURENCE. Long term.

FRANCES. Always?

The word catches LAURENCE *out. He considers for a second.*

LAURENCE. Yes. That.

FRANCES. So... what exactly are you proposing?

LAURENCE. Proposing?

FRANCES. Yes. What is the nature... of your proposal to me...?

LAURENCE *fights slightly shy...*

LAURENCE. I think I've made myself clear. Haven't I?

He lifts her hands and kisses both.

FRANCES. Wow.

LAURENCE. I'll tell the children. Tonight. Yeah. And why don't I pick you up later tonight? I'll stay off the hooch and we'll head straight off. A long weekend at Biddenbrooke to celebrate.

FRANCES. I hope there's Champagne in the fridge.

LAURENCE. Darling girl.

He hurries away. FRANCES *encounters* MARY *in the corridor…*

MARY. Oh – good, Frances. I wanted to ask you about…

But MARY *stops, noticing something.*

What's that? On your wedding finger…?

FRANCES. Oh – gosh… It's just my hairband. I took it out earlier and…

But MARY*'s on to something.*

MARY. I don't believe you.

MARY*'s phone rings – to her annoyance.*

Aaaagh. Hello, Mary Pym…? I'll be right through.

She hangs up, frustrated.

Robin. More 'synergies' and 'clicks' and 'traction', no doubt.

She gets a bunch of papers together.

You, young lady, are a dark horse. To be continued.

MARY *heads to* ROBIN*'s office.*

FRANCES (*out front*). But it isn't continued.

SID *hurries over, shocked, to where* FRANCES *is working.*

SID. What the fuck's happening?

He gestures to the scene unfolding in ROBIN*'s office, distressed…* MARY *is being fired.* FRANCES *keeps her voice low.*

FRANCES. I know… I feel awful. Robin asked where she was earlier – so I told him. At the osteopath. Then he asked about her Edinburgh expenses. He hadn't heard she took both kids along.

SID. You didn't.

FRANCES. They were quite big dinner bills.

SID. Frances…?

FRANCES. I'd feel worse, but the job was killing her. Leaving this place will put years on her life. People like us, we can take it… But Mary…?

MARY *is escorted out.* FRANCES *waves farewell.* SID *backs away from* FRANCES, *appalled.*

SID. Who are you?

But she rounds on him, unperturbed.

FRANCES. I'm Frances Thorpe and at the end of the day, I'll be announced as the new…

The penny drops for SID –

SID. Books Editor…

But FRANCES *swiftly corrects him –*

FRANCES. Arts Editor, actually. We're folding Books in.

SID. Arts…? But that's Michael's job. He's been here forever…

FRANCES. I know. It's sad. He just got too expensive – the pension, the BUPA payments. The good news is I'd like you on board as my deputy. Unless you're too busy with the screenplay. Think about it.

SID *struggles for a moment to process this, reels away, dazed.*

I go home and pack for the weekend.

A car beeps, then accelerates away.

It's a bit after ten when Laurence arrives. We begin the long drive to the Suffolk coast. He talks about his progress with the novel. He's asked Charlotte to read it as soon as it's done. Then he's quiet for a while. Until –

LAURENCE *comes in with his weekend bag, coat. We're at Biddenbrooke. He dumps them in a heap on the table.*

LAURENCE. *Really* sorry. The timing wasn't right. I'm going to make it up to you. I promise. Wait and see.

LAURENCE hurries back out, returns with a Thermos box.

FRANCES. They saw the photograph...?

LAURENCE. Yes. But I told them what you said – just two friends having dinner.

She just stares at him.

I think this cheese I brought is pretty good. I'll just grab the wine.

LAURENCE heads out again. FRANCES has had it now.

FRANCES. Where's his fucking phone?

She quickly locates it...

One, two, three, four.

FRANCES dials... after a short while –

POLLY *(voice-over)*. Hi, you've reached Polly... I'm clearly too fabulous to take your call. Please leave a message after the... Whoa – here it comes –

A beep. FRANCES sets the phone down on the table, calls:

FRANCES. Laurence...!

LAURENCE hurries back in with the wine, sheepish. He's relieved to find her on softer form –

I've been thinking about how you could make it up to me.

LAURENCE. Oh... really? Good...

She pulls him to her, kisses him deeply. LAURENCE is surprised, but thrilled.

The encounter swiftly escalates... FRANCES treats us to a series of marvellously performed little squeals and moans of pleasure. It's a prize-winning erotic assault. LAURENCE is thrilled.

The sound of frenzied shagging coming from a phone
speaker... The sound hits a crescendo, then – cuts to silence.
We hear nothing but birdsong. The most peaceful rural
dawn.

Chapter Twelve

The Biddenbrooke house, next morning.

FRANCES. I wake up happy, my head on Alys's feather pillow, her husband asleep beside me.

And I feel very close to her – perhaps as close as I've ever been, apart from that moment in the woods.

I hope she's happy for me. I am a different person now. Other people will be different too.

She's helped me see how nice people are overlooked, taken for granted.

FRANCES *addresses* ALYS *now.*

Oh, Alys. You really let things go. That's not going to happen on my watch.

Look at your china coffee-grinder, bolted on the pantry wall, your cherry-stoner, grape scissors. These things just break my heart.

LAURENCE *comes in.*

LAURENCE. You're very cheerful this morning...

FRANCES. I feel so at home here...

The doorbell rings. They're both surprised.

LAURENCE. I'll get rid of them. Whoever it is.

LAURENCE *goes off.* FRANCES *faces out –*

FRANCES. Wait for it –

> FRANCES *thrills at the scrunch of gravel, a car door being slammed, and* POLLY*'s voice, high and excited.*

POLLY (*offstage*). Wow, Dad, you need to work on your privacy settings. Your fucking phone.

LAURENCE (*offstage*). Darling, what do you mean...?

POLLY (*offstage*). Don't 'darling' me... She's here, isn't she... I know she is...

> POLLY *bursts in. Finds* FRANCES *waiting.*

I knew it... Unbelievable.

> LAURENCE *is close behind her...*

How could you?

FRANCES. Laurence – ?

POLLY. All the while pretending to be my friend...

LAURENCE. Polly, please...

> CHARLOTTE *and* TEDDY *arrive now...*

POLLY. How long has this been going on?

CHARLOTTE. Polly...

POLLY. How long?!

LAURENCE. A... a while.

POLLY. Jesus!

> POLLY *turns to* CHARLOTTE.

I told you it was true...

CHARLOTTE. But this isn't the way to deal with it.

LAURENCE. This is all my fault. I was going to tell you both last night. Frances said I should...

FRANCES. We wanted you to be the first to know.

She pulls close to LAURENCE… *A shiver round the room.*

POLLY. To know…?

FRANCES. As of yesterday. This isn't some… fling…

LAURENCE *is outfoxed as* FRANCES *slips his arm around her.*

LAURENCE. No. Exactly.

POLLY *staggers.*

TEDDY. You can't be serious.

CHARLOTTE. Darlings, your father's been very sad. Perhaps he shouldn't wait any longer to be happy…?

POLLY. But he didn't wait, did he?

TEDDY *senses trouble.*

CHARLOTTE. It's been over a year…

POLLY *can't help herself.*

POLLY. What about when Mum was still alive…?

POLLY *looks at her reluctant brother.*

Teddy knows all about it. Tell him, Teddy.

But TEDDY *won't…*

Fucking tell him!

But he won't. POLLY *goes it alone –*

You were having an affair. Mum found out. She drove off upset and she died.

LAURENCE. No… that's not what happened.

TEDDY. Jesus – don't make it worse, Dad. 'Julia Price'. I heard the whole thing.

LAURENCE *struggles, then –*

LAURENCE. Oh fuck. *Yes.*

TEDDY *exhales in horror and relief.* FRANCES *whimpers then covers her mouth.*

POLLY. Oh, so Frances didn't know about this. Not feeling so special now?

FRANCES. I didn't know, Polly. That is true…

And with perfect timing –

But surely, the question is… how did Alys find out?

The room is still for a moment as the family members wonder…

Wasn't she fine until she gave Charlotte that lift to the station? Isn't that what you said?

Everyone looks to CHARLOTTE.

LAURENCE. Charlotte…?

CHARLOTTE*'s mind reels.*

Charlotte…

CHARLOTTE. I will never forgive myself.

LAURENCE *can't believe it…*

LAURENCE. Why…?

CHARLOTTE. Because she knew there was *someone.* She had the initials 'JP', from the card, in that book you'd been given at Christmas. I confirmed the name.

She's angry with LAURENCE.

I was a friend to you both. I helped you more often than I should have. You were tormenting her!

LAURENCE *is deeply shocked. The children are exhausted. After a while…*

FRANCES. I feel I should leave.

LAURENCE. No –

He clutches her arm. POLLY *gets worryingly close to*
FRANCES, *looking at her as if for the first time.*

POLLY. God, where did you even come from?

FRANCES holds POLLY *in her gaze.* POLLY *storms out.*
TEDDY *looks at* FRANCES, *then follows his sister.*
CHARLOTTE *hovers, wringing her hands…*

CHARLOTTE. Laurence…

LAURENCE. Get out of the house.

CHARLOTTE. You can't imagine what I've been through…

TEDDY returns.

TEDDY. Charlotte, get in the car.

CHARLOTTE. But…

TEDDY suddenly erupts –

TEDDY. Get the fuck in or we're going without you.

She leaves with him, distraught. The sound of a car leaving.
LAURENCE *is dazed. Slumps into a chair, head in hands.*

LAURENCE. What a terrible way for them to find out…

FRANCES. How did they?

LAURENCE. I didn't lock my bloody phone, I must have
knocked it when we were… well, anyway, it dialled Polly's
number, she overheard us.

FRANCES affects shock.

FRANCES. Oh no.

Then recovers.

Of course, this wasn't really about us…

LAURENCE. No. You're right. God. Julia Price. One slip, one
mistake…

FRANCES faces out.

FRANCES. One slip. Great with words. Not good with numbers.

LAURENCE. I want you to know everything. I was never
    going to leave Alys. I promised her I'd end it, and I did. Just
    the thought of that woman makes me sick.

FRANCES. You'll have to cut Charlotte loose, you know.

LAURENCE *is wild-eyed at the prospect.*

LAURENCE. Oh, Christ…

FRANCES. To have any hope of saving your relationship with
    the children.

LAURENCE. I don't think they'll ever forgive me.

FRANCES. Of course they will.

LAURENCE. No. They're stubborn… Judgemental. We ruined
    them both. Let them drift through life with no sense of how
    it really works.

FRANCES. They're young.

LAURENCE. Not that young. By the time I was their age…

FRANCES. And they've taken a lot for granted, but they'll
    soon see that.

He leans in to her, grateful.

LAURENCE. God, if they had half your get-up-and-go.

She considers a moment.

FRANCES. We should change the locks here.

LAURENCE. What…?

FRANCES. So many people have let themselves in down the
    years. And after that business at Christmas.

LAURENCE *doesn't like it, but accepts this.*

LAURENCE. I suppose you're right.

FRANCES. At the London house, too. Put things with the kids on a fresh footing. A chance to redraw the boundaries. That's the way to start again.

LAURENCE *rubs his face.*

LAURENCE. Christ, what a mess.

FRANCES. Change is always messy. Now. We're going to pull ourselves together. And get on with our day. I have several books to read. And you have one to write.

LAURENCE *accepts this, hesitates only a moment before...*

LAURENCE. Darling, I have a huge favour to ask...

FRANCES. Of course. Anything.

LAURENCE. When I get to the end of this first draft... Is there any chance you'd take a look?

FRANCES *is overwhelmed. Takes his face in her hands for a moment, then kisses his forehead. LAURENCE is satisfied, potters off, grateful. Back to the desk.*

FRANCES *faces out.*

FRANCES. I'm not a writer, like Laurence. But I grasp the mechanics of plot. 'Dear Polly... Dear Teddy. You've no idea how much he misses you. He won't give up on you,' I write. 'And nor will I.'

FRANCES *wraps her arms around herself for a moment, as the salt breeze blows through.*

I've invited Robin and his wife for supper in London. He and I actually get on quite well.

I'll have Mrs King prepare Alys's sea bass with samphire, I think. And perhaps her lovely panna cotta. I'll do the flowers myself. Order them, I mean.

As for Laurence and me. And what the future holds...

FRANCES *cradles her belly in a clear suggestion. But then – refutes it –*

I haven't quite decided yet.

She takes us in.

Frances. With an 'e'.

Can you see me now?

Ends.

www.nickhernbooks.co.uk

facebook.com/nickhernbooks

twitter.com/nickhernbooks